Still
Christian
After All These
Years

Still Christian After All These Years

Barbara Allen

A

JourneyBook

from

Church Publishing Incorporated New York

Library of Congress Cataloging-in-Publication Data

Allen, Barbara.
Still Christian after all these years / Barbara Allen.
    p. cm. - (JourneyBook)
ISBN: 0-89869-400-0 (pbk.)

                       2003062538

JourneyBook and colophon are registered trademarks of Church Publishing Incorporated
Designed by Betty Mintz

Church Publishing Incorporated
445 Fifth Avenue
New York, NY 10016
www.churchpublishing.org

5 4 3 2 1

To my husband, Bill,
who said those three little words: Take your time.

Acknowledgments

I want to thank my priest and friend, Gray Temple, and my "believing mirrors": Sharon Anderson, Nancy Dusenberry, Kathy Holman, Janet Griffin, Katherine McCabe, Dee Dee Risher, Pam Smith, and Linda Sommer.

Introduction

IF YOU'RE LUCKY, you're born into a faith you can live with and die with: faith of our fathers, good enough for mother, homegrown and all spelled out. If you're even luckier, it all falls apart somewhere along the line, and you have to start from scratch. You trim, adjust, weigh, discern and ponder until you have...what? Perhaps a faith that knows little, but knows it deeply.

The change in your religious perceptions is often gradual, like skin sloughing off in tiny flakes. You barely know what is happening. Only in retrospect do you see how you have redefined Christian fellowship, profoundly changed your view of God, and found a faith that fits better, like finally wearing the right clothes for the first time.

Why do some people believe so easily and others of us have to find our way, reading and searching and re-examining as we go? Did some Episcopalian gypsies leave me on the doorstep of Baptist missionaries? Is there spiritual life after fundamentalism? Do the people who are 100 percent certain, who have all their doctrinal specifics nailed down to the last jot and tittle, have a corner on the Christian faith? Or does faith not have much truck with certainty?

If you sat in church as a youngster, wearing your perfect attendance pin, while other believers around you popped up with testimonies, recounting experiences of direct revelation ("The Lord said to me...") while your Lord is silent or out to lunch, it's no wonder you doubt your salvation and, occasionally, your sanity. You're surrounded by good people who seem to bounce along like merry bubbles, reassuring each other and rejoicing in their "inness" while you wonder, "What am I doing here?" Are they reading a different Bible? Am I not praying hard enough? Or are they sometimes faking it too?

An old country preacher used to say that we have trouble because we are building a cottage while God's blueprint calls for us to build a mansion. But I'm from the Midwest, where we have modest aspirations. I prefer a cottage, snug and manageable. Mansions are drafty. And, if remodeling is called for, I like to do it gradually. No, that wallpaper doesn't quite work after all. How about trying the piano over *here*? Then, as Anne Lamott says in *Traveling Mercies: Some Thoughts on Faith,* "You look out the window and here comes Jesus with a wrecking ball."

Even looking back, I don't see any way I could have envisioned the broad and joyful "mansion" that is my life today. Nobody around me lived in one, metaphorical or otherwise. Nobody expected to either. Quite the opposite, to be a Christian was to be humble, quiet and to take the lowest part. As Garrison Keillor said, when *Prairie Home Companion* was broadcast from Hawaii, "My people are not paradise people." Maybe that trait of having low expectations is one reason I never even staked out the foundation of my mansion and averted my eyes from any royal vision that crept in sideways. But I did foster and treasure each cottage along the way, and maybe it was grace and hope that gave me the energy and colors to rebuild when each one fell or burned or exploded.

So am I a Christian? Yes, but I prefer the word believer. The term Christian only leads to more categories: Born-again? Spirit-filled? Spirit-baptized? How can I look at my life, evaluate it and bring out the parts that say, "She's definitely a Christian." Aha! You see? That proves it! I can't. The tapestry of my life isn't so fine and strong to stand picking at. What do I know for sure? Not much.

I know something inside told me from the very beginning that the people around me had a kernel of the truth, but their truth didn't match my experience of God. Although we talked about a personal relationship with Jesus, said that was paramount, the litmus test, our life in community, was spent emphasizing a code, a lifestyle that made *us* unique, better, and *them*, the unbelievers, objects of scorn or pity. In fact, it may have been the emphasis on the difference that made me wonder whether I was one of them or one of us or neither. I felt a bond with certain people, but it wasn't based on doctrinal correctness or similar beliefs. The bond depended more on whether I enjoyed them, trusted them. Some were Christians, and some weren't. Some were even Methodists.

Once a week during kindergarten, I went after school to Child Evangelism Fellowship, a time in someone's home when we had wonderful flannel-board Bible stories, songs and even sometimes, oh, joy, crafts. As soon as I walked into the house, my first glance would be at the dining room table where, if it were a crafts day, there would be little individual piles of material laid out for our project: a plaster of Paris Scripture verse plaque or a picture of Jesus cradling a lamb (us) to be colored and framed in Popsicle sticks. We were expected, planned for, invited as honored guests. What a treat! But one song, done with motions, stands out in my mind.

> One door and only one
> and yet its sides are two.
> I'm on the inside!
> On which side are you?

What did it mean? Were we welcome, pampered guests because we were on the inside? Were we on the outside but being invited in? What if I couldn't be sure I was on the inside or that anyone who wasn't like us was on the outside? Or was it that door, that ONE door, that barrier tall and solid, which only admitted certain ones who had it right, who bore witness to a personal relationship with Jesus Christ and kept out all others? I tried to picture Jesus, the Good Shepherd, going around the room, standing in front of each one of us, saying, "Yes, yes, no, yes, no." Not sure? Slam! Catholic? Slam!

The Scripture, I saw, was clear: only one mediator, one door, one Savior, who died once for all. But while I did believe this, did accept Christ, the one, that one door, the image of we're in and you're out...something didn't ring true. Even at five, I knew I loved the Lord but hated that door. I wanted to kick it.

But I kept quiet about my feelings because doubt was not our way. Once in high school, I confided to a youth minister, telling him that sometimes I wasn't sure I was a Christian. I don't remember his answer. But I do remember clearly the next Sunday night when he announced to the whole young people's group that Barbara isn't sure she's a Christian. Stare, stare. He probably went on to speak about the assurance of one's salvation. All I learned that night was to keep my doubts to myself if I didn't want to be next week's sermon illustration.

How does grace break through a cramped, lonely childhood when the outsiders are suspect at best but home isn't so safe either? Sometimes the World, ungodly and always capitalized, looked so fine and inviting, but, of course, they said it always did at the beginning. How could I wholeheartedly embrace a belief when its restrictions made my teen years socially isolated, when the church urged me to be different and outspoken at a time I desperately wanted to quietly belong?

It's been a long trip. I started at the far right end of Protestantism, attended a fundamentalist university and experienced a long and painful marriage to a Baptist minister. I have ended up an Episcopalian, happily paired with a Catholic dropout. Oh, me.

Still Christian after all these years.

Section I • The Early Forties

"Liar, Liar"

I WAS FIVE THE SUMMER I LIED. About once a week, my folks would leave me with one of two teenage babysitters, neighbors. Moira was my favorite, part of a wonderful Scottish clan who lived next door. She let me have all her "junk" when she cleaned out her dresser drawers, and she always smelled of Cashmere Bouquet.

I learned a lot from Moira: how to make piles of cut grass to jump in and then redistribute it because her dad told us to leave it where it was; how to put red nail polish on your glasses frames for a "new look." I learned when you lie out for a tan, you have to protect your nose from getting burned because it's closest to the sun. I'd sit on her piano bench next to her and dream about romance while she played and sang "Because" from sheet music with a bride and groom silhouetted on the front. I imagined being her flower girl, in a dress that was an exact miniature of her bridal gown. She cut my bangs and did my hair in a page-boy style like June Allyson, and afterward, for the rest of the day, I wouldn't make any quick moves with my head for fear of messing it up. Mom asked if I had a sore neck.

Susan was the other sitter. She was beautiful too, dark with freckles, but she sort of ignored me and talked on the phone while she leafed through the movie magazines she'd brought along. (We'd never have such a thing in our house, just *Moody Monthly* and last week's Sunday school papers). One day she asked me if Moira had a boyfriend. I said no and felt her attention waning, so blurted out, "She says you're stuck up!" Instant focus. "What else does she say about me?" I'd used up the only phrase I knew from teenage gossip, so I grabbed through my mind for something else to make up from scratch. "She says you fell and broke your arm!"

I don't remember how the parents got involved in this, but my mom said I had to go down to Susan's house and say I lied and apologize. We lived at the top of a small, steep dirt road, lined with houses on both sides. Elizabeth Court dead-ended at the bottom, where the Black River flowed. I was never allowed to go near there, and had been warned against it so much that I pictured the river as literally black—swirling, foamy and treacherous, maybe even with tidal waves that would reach up and get you. Susan lived at the end of the street in the house next to the river.

As I started down the hill, I began to cry. Not only had I lied but I had lied about my good friend, Moira. By the time I'd mounted the stairs, pulling myself up by the banister, and rung the doorbell, I was holding onto the doorframe, sobbing with shame and remorse. Susan's mother opened the door. Without preamble, I blurted out, "I lied! I lied! I'm sorry!" If she was puzzled about my outburst, she didn't let on, didn't question me. I knew the moms had discussed my transgression. She brought me right in. Would I like some lemonade? The sobs slowly subsided to hiccups. Another woman, maybe Susan's aunt or grandmother, seated me like an honored guest in a small platform rocker next to a bay window looking out on the river below. I could hardly see through my hot, swollen eyelids. Amazing! It was a gentle little river, with woods along the banks. Water danced over mossy rocks, sunlight sparkled on little swirls and eddies and waterfalls, clear and green. It was shallow enough to wade across! A flat rock in the middle looked just right for a tea party picnic.

The women brought in a tray with real lemonade in a frosty glass pitcher, like the one on the Kool-Aid package, and real glass glasses, filled with ice cubes. They put the tray on a table covered with a lace tablecloth. I never knew for sure what the women looked like, because I never raised my eyes up from the rug, except to look out the window. It was like a dream, the hostesses, graceful as ballerinas, the fan overhead making a gentle breeze, the beautiful view, the tinkly ice and sweet, tart lemonade. My hiccups stopped.

Down the Yellow Brick Road

I REMEMBER MY FIRST REAL BIRTHDAY PARTY where I got to wear my Sunday dress on Saturday and take a present, wrapped. My dad dropped me off at the house, but once inside, the parents said, "Don't take off your coats. We have a surprise." We're going to a movie! I thought these people were Christians! They go to our church, don't they?

I had never been to a movie. It's a sin that ranks right up there with dancing, smoking and "running around," whatever that is. We don't even look at the pictures outside the theater. Who knows what you might see and who might see you looking. Besides if you get close enough, something could just suck you right in.

My mind swirled. We were bundled into a car and headed to town. It was 1944, and Judy Garland was starring in *The Wizard of Oz*. While they parked, I stood on tiptoe to get a good look at the woman in the fortuneteller booth selling tickets. In spite of being a tool of the devil, she looked normal, just bored and wearing too much make-up. Inside I noticed each usher, too, in their braided jackets and caps. What kind of person would work every day in this darkened, exotic den of iniquity? Does that explain the pimples, the pallor?

But the place was magnificent: high ceilings and pillars and gold fixtures, like a post office with popcorn. I sank back into my cushioned seat, slid down and took it all in. This was my chance! Then the red velvet curtains hummed open and the movie started. I was transported. My little image-starved soul, oh! Water on a desert. My heart nearly burst with the terror of the tornado, the beauty of Oz…. And then, halfway through the movie, someone shouted, "Fire!" We all pushed and shoved to get out in a hurry. I pictured flames leaping around the exit, trapping us inside and knew I was going straight to hell. And I never even got to go to kindergarten. But we saw no evidence of a fire, just a bad smell from something amiss in the projection room and, after a short huddle on the cold sidewalk, we were herded back in.

. . . . . .

I'd never be the same after my brief detour off the straight and narrow. An innocent birthday invitation opened vistas I could never have imagined on my own in a world before television. Just around the corner from our church was a movie theater, window to the world of wonder and drama and sophistication. So near and yet so far away.

SEX EDUCATION *AL FRESCO*

I DON'T REMEMBER where we got the name for our club, Daughters of the Moon. We probably heard the phrase somewhere and liked the sound of it. It sounded exotic and far away from our little dead-end dirt street. There were just the three of us, two Barbaras and one Joyce. Our club mainly came about because we'd discovered a private and secret place under the willow tree. We could see out, but nobody could see us. A willow in full bright-green leaf makes a wonderful hiding place, and you could even be dry when it rained and your mom was calling from the porch, while you pretended not to hear.

From our safe vantage point we could see all that happened in our little neighborhood, which wasn't much. A dad waiting at the bus stop with his lunch pail. Bunches of big kids, hugging their schoolbooks and shoving each other off the sidewalk. We giggled at Mrs. Wilson's funny Sears undies hung out to dry, including a stiff, bony corset which, when unhooked and opened all the way, took up half the clothesline. We could watch the Fuller Brush man, the mailman, the milkman do their rounds. The strange, doughy lady who rented an upstairs room from the Kirkpatricks would let down her Maxwell House coffee can with the sock hanging next to it. The milkman would take the money out of the sock, exchange a bottle of milk for the empty one, and she'd haul it back up.

If a robber came, we'd be ready. Thinking the coast was clear, he'd crawl in a window, and we'd be the only eyewitnesses. "Yes, sir, he wore a blue cap and had a mustache, and we scratched his license plate number in the dirt right here." "Oh, it was nine or ten o'clock. On the dot!" Maybe there'd be a reward and we could buy the new Katy Keene paper dolls. Meantime we decided on a Kool-Aid stand.

We set up for business on the corner and sold Kool-Aid for five cents a glass. This was before paper cups were common, so we had a dishpan under the card table to wash the used glasses. Mean, snooty Robert Zacharia walked over from across the street just to point out loudly that this wasn't "sanitary," so I told his mom he said a bad word. When we divided up the money under the willow tree, there was one penny left over, which stumped us for a while until we decided to give it to my Mom since she'd given us the Kool-Aid and sugar and ice.

But the main business of the Daughters of the Moon was to learn about sex. We exchanged misinformation on a regular basis. My specialty was the penis, because I was the only one who knew anything for sure, and the rest I could make up.

It wasn't that my Baptist parents had told me anything. Once I had to go to the bathroom very badly, and my dad was taking a bath. So my mother took me in and said to him, "We'll look in the opposite direction." All I learned that day was what "opposite" meant.

I was friends with a boy in our neighborhood, and I went over one day to ask him out to play. He said he had to go to the bathroom first, so I waited in the living room while he went upstairs. He didn't close the bathroom door, so I heard the stream of pee go pssssst (stop), pssssst (stop), pssssst. When I peed, it was just one long pssssst, so something was very different there.

Somewhere, maybe in an encyclopedia or doctor's office, I had had a very brief glimpse of a drawing of a man, and my impression was that there were two parts, a front part, tube-like, and a second part, a sac-like something behind. I put this information together with my mother's perfume atomizer and decided boys' sacs must fill up with pee, then they squeeze the sac, and pee spritzes out of the tip of the tube in front. Pssssst (stop), pssssst (stop), pssssst. I explained this to my friends, drawing a diagram with my finger in the dirt.

We learned a lot under that willow tree. And wondered about a lot more. What was Kirkpatrick's mysterious boarder really like? Had she once been young and beautiful, but her only love died in World War I so that she went a little mad? Why did Becker's dad never go to work? Where did Mrs. Yost get the money to go shopping every day? We still wondered a lot about sex too, how babies started and where they actually came from. But the Daughters of the Moon knew all we needed to know about the penis.

Art Appreciation

MY CHRISTIAN CHILDHOOD in the forties was a feast for the ears, but a famine for the eyes. At church the other senses were fed. We heard rousing sermons and full-bodied music: choirs of all ages, crisp, bright trumpet solos, men's quartets and ladies' trios. In Sunday school we learned hundreds of choruses by heart, all the verses, with accompanying motions. Once, during revival, we had a black group called the Jubilee Singers, with a bass who was built like a refrigerator. He made the unstained windows shake. (When the appeal went out for homes to host the singers, I asked my mom if we could invite him, but she said, "What would the neighbors think?") Sunday morning church smells were a clean, comfortable mixture of Midnight in Paris, shoe polish and the meat loaf from last night's fellowship potluck.

Our house was as plain as our church. A few low-maintenance evergreen shrubs left by the last owners grew outside. Interior décor consisted of neutral wallpaper, white sheers at every window and tan wall-to-wall carpeting. Since there was no color to tire of or style to go out of, nothing was changed until it wore out, only to be replaced with similar stuff. It never occurred to us that even "all things in moderation" could be taken to extremes.

Once, when my parents were ordering new carpeting for the living room, I wondered aloud if it had to be tan again. The next day at dinner, Mom announced triumphantly in my direction that, as a matter of fact, for my information, the new carpet wouldn't be tan. What color would it be? "Coffee!"

Sometimes on our walk home after school, I sneaked into the Catholic church with my friend Kathy, who was Catholic. It was next door to the jail, so first we would stand on the sidewalk in front of the jail, look up to the barred windows on the second floor, shade our eyes and shout, "Hope you get out soon, Dad!"

"WHAT?"

. . . . .

"Yeah, I'll come visit you tomorrow!" Then we'd bend over laughing.

I loved that Kathy's church was always open. Our church, called the Church of the Open Door, was always locked except for services. St. Mary's, as we came in blinking from the sunny afternoon, assailed the senses: cold holy water in the stone basin, the pungent, smoky aroma of incense, candles burning, deep, vibrant colors streaming through the stained glass windows onto golden triptychs and statues of all shapes and sizes. I knew it was wrong to worship idols, but it was all so elegant and exotic. I would not have been surprised to see elephants processing down the aisle.

In order to keep our church pure from idol worship, we avoided any form of icons. The only picture was a colored pencil rendering of the church building itself. The drawing included rose bushes, which were either part of the original plan or a touch of artistic license. Flowers were a part of nature, so that extravagance would have been okay, but no one ever planted them. In any case, the front of the church stayed plain except for the sign-board with a weekly admonition from the Scripture and the double steel doors, locked. It was a single-story, multi-purpose building with crank-out windows and a modest steeple. No one could say we were prideful.

Art in general was not simply absent, it was downright suspect. How could artists be Christians? They were messy, independent, Bohemian and unorthodox. They drove vans and slept late. We drove Buicks and went to the barber every Saturday morning.

The single exception to this mistrust of art was chalk artists, who came to our beige cinderblock church during spring and fall revivals. What a treat to my little color-starved soul! I could hardly wait. I sat in the front row. The lights went down, a spotlight focused on the broad blank canvas, the organ music swelled, and he would start. As the artist swayed back and forth, a landscape and billowy clouds would begin to appear before our eyes, sweeping waves of color, swoops and loops! What drama! What magic!

. . . . . .

The end result was always the same: Calvary at sunset. Three stark, black, empty crosses on a hill.

When the artist finished, he would stand back and turn on a light with a color wheel. While the organ played "The Old Rugged Cross," the picture would slowly change colors. The blue light turned the beautiful, lonely scene cold and stark.

> On a hill far away,
> Stood an old, rugged cross,

Blue faded slowly into purple, then violet, then red, warm and bloody. I was there at Calvary, where the Lord was dying for me, where the dazzling world he'd made came to a standstill and all creation mourned. My heart nearly broke with grief and love.

> The emblem of suffering and shame.

Red into orange and then yellow, golden and bright with resurrection glory.

> But I loved that old cross,
> Where the dearest and best
> For a world of lost sinners was slain.

In the end, the drawing was presented to the lucky person who had brought the most visitors. It was never me.

So we went home to a house with three pieces of art: a plaque on the kitchen wall, a varnished, diagonal slice of redwood from California, etched with a verse which merrily greeted us every morning at breakfast:

. . . . . .

>Only one life,
>'Twill soon be past.
>Only what's done
>For Christ will last.

The other two works of art were both in the living room, with the new coffee carpeting: praying hands and Sallman's pale, blue-eyed *Head of Christ,* which I knew to be authentic because it had been painted by King Solomon himself.

. . . . . .

The Ice Cream Boycott

WHERE WAS DAD? When I think back to my childhood, at home or at family get-togethers, I can't picture him, can't hear his voice. I know he was there. Born-again dads didn't drink, smoke or gamble, and they came straight home after work. But I can only picture him behind his newspaper.

My mom's family were all extroverts, dark and intense, always on the phone or talking over the fence: busy people. Dad was fair, thin and quiet. Mom's sisters were merciless teases when they noticed me at all. I was never to call them "aunt" because that would make them feel old. Since I never had any affection from them or for them, that was easy.

Because my folks had been Baptist Home Missionaries in Kentucky until I was about four, my aunts said I should be able to yodel like a hillbilly. "Come on! Let's hear you yodel!" If I cried or ran away, it showed I wasn't a "good sport." When I came home from school and spotted one of their cars in the drive, I stayed outside.

I dreaded Sunday afternoon gatherings at Grandpa Keiffer's. It meant long, boring hours of staying out of the way while the Cleveland Indians were on the radio in the living room and the women gossiped in the kitchen. An old Chinese checkerboard in the cupboard was the sole concession to children being present.

On occasion, someone would go to the store for ice cream, a real treat before anyone had home freezers. My grandpa would call out, "Oh, boy! Ice cream!" But when we kids came running, he'd turn and say, "What do *you* want? Who invited *you*?" One Sunday I came with the others and, when he said, "Who asked *you*? What do *you* want?" I said I didn't want anything and turned to leave. He said, "Oh, I was just kidding," and held out some ice cream. But I said I didn't care for any, thank you. That's when the roof fell in. Oh, the chaos! The consternation! Of course you want some. He was just teasing. Can't you take a joke?

. . . . . .

What's the matter with you? But I was adamant. I didn't want his ice cream. Shame on you! What's wrong with you? Be a sport! Now take it, it's chocolate! It's your favorite flavor! No, thank you.

By now everyone had turned on me. But something inside had clicked. I was tired of this loud guy with his hard laugh, his Chiclet-looking dentures, this stupid joke. And mad at myself for falling for it again. Nobody ever paid much attention to me; why couldn't they just let this drop? I hadn't hit anyone or told a lie. Maybe I wanted to save my pride for a change, to say I was a person too. And a scoop of chocolate ice cream was a small price to pay. But some code had been broken, a speeding train derailed. So, instead of just being slightly naughty or overly sensitive or disrespectful, I was a disgrace, the focus of common wrath, scorn and outrage. It was unanimous. I was a brush fire that had to be stamped out.

I didn't understand this family, the Keiffers or my dad—the different one. My friends' dads were mostly genial fellows who raked the lawn, smoked pipes and went bowling. They were friendly and approachable. The Polish man across the street, Andy Jeseski, who had fought in World War II, put up a flag every morning before he drove off in his square white milk truck and took it down each night. He and his wife had five handsome sons who went straight from Catholic high school graduation into some branch of the service, and they had pictures of each of them in uniform displayed in the living room. Afternoons, Mr. J. merrily kept his yard and garden immaculate, growing flowers in front and enough tomatoes in back for the whole neighborhood. One day we watched from our porch as two men in dark suits came up and talked to him while he was watering his lawn. After a long talk, we were amazed to see him turn the hose on them! We found out later they were Jehovah's Witnesses who told him his flag was an idol, an abomination to the Lord, and that he should take it down. He disagreed and, when they persisted, he calmly spritzed them, Bibles and all, off his property.

My best friend, Anne, had a dad who owned a small nursery and yard service. Ted

Carpenter's workers were from West Virginia or Kentucky, men who had come up to work at the steel mill and then got laid off. One of Ted's workers had a young daughter who died, and he wanted to take her body home to be buried, but he couldn't afford a hearse. Mr. Carpenter wanted to drive the casket down in his pick-up truck, but the authorities said it was illegal. So he called the Sheriff and laid it out. Told him he was leaving the next morning at seven, taking the coffin to Kentucky. He'd be traveling south on Route 57. Two police cars were waiting at the on ramp. Ted kept driving and one car went ahead and one behind, escorting him to the state line, where they turned back and Kentucky police silently took over.

What kind of father does this? What would it feel like to have the kind of dad who sticks up for what he believes in and doesn't care what people think? I didn't know the phrase civil disobedience, but I knew valor when I saw it. My dad was a Baptist, a Christian, and we obeyed all rules, took no chances, colored inside the lines. Our Christian duty was to be model citizens and jail anyone who wasn't. People who went against the tide, spoke out, demonstrated, were just asking for trouble. When someone we knew joined a televised march against drugs, Dad pointed out that the dealers could be watching and could find out where you lived. You'd never catch him doing something that foolish!

I remember all the Keiffers so clearly the day of my ice cream boycott: clenched jaws, hands on their wide hips, indignant and put out. I remember their bright eyes and angry, scowling faces. I remember the smell of smoke and aftershave, pot roast and coffee. But where was Dad?

In my imagination, he folds up his newspaper, steps into the kitchen and puts his hand on my shoulder. "Actually, Bar's never cared much for chocolate. We'll walk down to the corner and get strawberry!" Just this once, he goes against the tide, loves me enough to protect and defend me. The others will shake their heads and say he's going to spoil me. But, for the moment, we don't care what they think. We walk in Sunday silence to the store.

. . . . . .

The Oceanfront Mansion

THERE WERE THREE OF US girl cousins growing up together in the forties, one year apart. I was the oldest, as was my mom, Judy was next, Evelyn's daughter, then Janice, Lois' girl, was the youngest. But we didn't like to play with Judy. No matter that she had the best of everything, the latest toys and even was allowed to wear patent leather shoes to school, she'd sit on the front steps and pout until her face, by the time she was ten, had a permanent "cheated" look, mouth drawn down, and big, sad brown eyes, restless, casting about to find something else that others had that she didn't. My mom and Lois had a quick way to stop us anytime Janice or I complained. "You sound like Judy!"

Janice was the opposite, sunny and giggly, even though she had an awfully shifty life. Her mom had several marriages and affairs and disappeared completely for long periods of time, so she stayed with us a lot. Janice and I had good imaginations and needed very little to make high drama in our boring little town of Elyria. Our best project one summer was Buy-A-Mansion—a plan I hatched in Atlantic City.

My dad was from Atlantic City, and we'd drive there each June to visit his dad (both my grandmothers died before I was born) and all his relatives—various siblings, cousins, aunts and uncles. What a contrast to Elyria! In this crowded, noisy inner-city neighborhood, I'd wake up to exotic smells of ethnic cooking and sounds of produce and seafood vendors in the street. I could have run outside and bought a banana for my breakfast if I'd had the nerve. Of course, I didn't. Instead, I watched the spectacle from an upstairs bedroom window, leaning my chin on the sill that was peeling in the salty ocean air. The neighborhood kids, including herds of my New Jersey cousins, were loud and wild-acting, outside in their pajamas, boisterous and bold. They scared me, but I envied their belonging-ness, their big city ways and their ready access to this grandpa I only got to see once a year. Grandpa Ross called the woman across the street, "the old lady who lived in a shoe," because she had so

18

many children. I loved it—an adult gossiping with me!

When we arrived, Grandpa Ross would pretend not to recognize me since I'd grown so much. "This can't be Barbara!" In his row house, there were two pianos no one ever played, one in the living room and one in the parlor. He'd take me over to the one with my pictures on top and show me myself as littler, what he'd expected.

The best part of going to Atlantic City was watching my dad, a sad, gray man at home, be the star. Here, the first-born, he was called "Willie," and was loved, was somebody. On Sunday, Aunt Geneva would bring over her clam chowder (with her Jersey accent, clam had two syllables, clay-um), and other relatives would drift in, awkward and diffident at first, but glad to see us. There was no mention of church and, when my grandpa died when I was thirteen, his lodge fellows held the funeral.

The family of one of Dad's old friends from seminary had an ice cream parlor, and we could order anything we wanted for free. I still remember my first banana split served in a clear oblong dish lined with banana halves, a big round scoop of strawberry ice cream in the middle, drizzled with strawberries. On one side was chocolate ice cream and hot fudge, on the other, vanilla with crushed pineapple. The whole thing was topped with real whipped cream, crushed nuts and three maraschino cherries with stems. And, as long as I'm on food, there was a place on the Boardwalk next to the Steel Pier that made forty kinds of donuts right there in the window. At home we had brown and white.

My dad grew up there under very hard circumstances—he was the oldest of six, only ten when his mother died. When the Depression hit, his dad, who had real estate holdings, lost everything. One great uncle committed suicide. The family moved often in this city that had become the Monopoly board, hopping from North Carolina Avenue to Marvin Gardens, seemingly at random, according to a toss of the dice. My dad would drive us along the ocean front in our old blue Buick to show us row after row of beautiful mansions, white as wedding cakes, with turrets, widows' walks and glassed-in sleeping porches with striped awnings.

He'd say that, during the Depression, if you had just a little cash put aside (not in banks, which failed and locked their doors), you could have bought any one of these spectacular homes. That one...or that one. But nobody had any money. Even the school children's savings account books were worthless overnight. So the houses stood empty. Nobody could even pay the taxes. Just imagine owning that one...or that one.

I decided then and there to start saving and never ever put my money in a bank. If Janice and I each saved our allowances, just a quarter a week, for, let's see...well, okay a long time, but still! Next time the banks failed, we'd be ready! We could move to Atlantic City and live in an oceanfront mansion and eat forty kinds of donuts for breakfast. If we saved each week, faithfully, and never spent our money, squandered it when the ice cream truck came ding-a-ling down the street, just imagine!

We washed out a mayonnaise jar and tried to dig a hole in the trashy, narrow space between our garage and the neighbor's garage. But the dirt was hard, and we only had a snow shovel. Our two quarters looked awfully small in that big jar, and we couldn't dig a hole that big anyway. So we got a jelly jar instead and, after bending several spoons, dug a small hole with a spatula. There! We'd started. No matter what happened: fire, earthquake, flood, atomic bomb, stock market crash, our small fortune, row after row of jelly and pickle and peanut butter jars filled with quarters, real cash money, would be safe underground, maybe the only U.S. currency left in Ohio! We swore each other to secrecy, patted down the dirt and waited for disaster to strike.

The second week we backslid. It was so hot and the orange Popsicles were delicious. And then, since we'd blown our allowances anyway, we dug up our mansion stash and bought fudgesicles too. We'd start again next week for sure. Won't it be wonderful? White curtains billowing in the ocean breezes, hot deck chairs, big beach umbrellas, wicker furniture, an outside shower over wooden slats to get off the sand and salt water. Everyone would be poor but us, and we'd only invite people to live with us we really liked. Not Judy.

· · · · · ·

Section II · Late Forties

Boarders

WE HAD THREE BEDROOMS: my parents', my brother's and mine. When my parents decided to rent out my bedroom, I was to move into a room in the attic. It was a small room, semi-finished, but very sunny, and smelled cleanly of mothballs. It had a slanted ceiling on either side, pale green dry wall and a linoleum floor. I was delighted. Being on the third floor meant privacy, autonomy, and refuge from the chaos below. I pictured having a tea party for my friends and, later, in high school, pajama parties. Maybe even boys and records, as long as we didn't dance.

I was in the fourth or fifth grade, but it made me feel independent and grown up, like having my very own apartment. Nobody I knew lived in an apartment, which would have been so citified and sophisticated compared to just living in a house with a scraggly patch of lawn. Apartments were high up in the clouds and had doormen to hail your cab; apartments were for New Yorkers and movie stars. Maybe I would even tape up pictures of movie stars on the walls. We never went to the movies, of course, but the covers of my school tablets had autographed pictures of women with flawless skin, dreamy eyes, long lashes, bowed red lips and high cheekbones. Stars. With apartments.

I don't remember what kind of bed they put up for me. In my regular bedroom, I had either twin beds or a double bed, depending on how my parents were getting along.

The room in the attic was pleasant, but the stairs leading up to it were dark and nasty. A dim, bare bulb hung over unpainted stairs, dusty and cluttered with piles of stuff to take up on your next trip. But each time you went into the attic, it was because you were already taking stuff up. I wanted it to look nice, so I could be proud to take my friends up. I got an old can of gray porch paint from the basement, broke through the skin and started painting

· · · · ·

the stairs. I hadn't thought to wash them first and was impatient to finish before I got caught, so I just painted fast, right over the dust and grime. When four or five stairs were done, I realized I couldn't reach the rest and should have started at the top. I don't remember whether someone caught me or I lost interest, but for the next twenty years that my parents lived there, only the bottom attic stairs were painted. Badly.

I loved having boarders. It was like having company, saying, "Good morning," and, "Please pass the salt," and my parents couldn't yell at each other.

My favorite boarder was Bella. She had long, bouncy black hair and big-front cashmere sweaters and lots of dates. She would come out of the bathroom in a cloud of Tabu, looking so glamorous. Boys drove by and tooted, and she'd run out and jump in the convertible, just like Veronica in the Archie comics. I adored her and envied her and decided she must be Catholic.

Of course, the next morning, she'd always oversleep and have to rush to use the only bathroom and get to work on time. The whole household would be in a frenzy by the time she exploded out the front door, like Dagwood, to catch the bus.

One day she was so late she was nearly in tears, and she told me to run down to the corner and hold the bus for her. I was so proud she needed me! I ran as fast as I could and frantically hailed the first bus I saw. The huge hulk pulled over and ground to a halt. I turned around to wave her on, only to see her stop in disgust. I had hailed a Greyhound.

Could I ever change from a skinny kid in a second-hand Brownie outfit into a grown-up young woman with boys honking out front? Not a chance. We didn't even associate with people like Bella with her overt sex appeal and wild life style. It was just by sheer luck, by some turn of events in our cash flow, that I even got a glimpse of such a lovely creature from another world, another life.

· · · · · ·

Cloutless in Ohio

FALL WAS MY FAVORITE. Kresge's dime store featured "Back to School" sales with prices written in white on fake blackboards and pencil boxes stacked in a pyramid in the window. It was in the air: kid-time, new shoes, hair cuts, lunch boxes. It was the thing to do, what all good parents did. So we joined the parade downtown to buy new notebooks, paper, some bright red socks, and underwear, always white. After September, Kresge's started celebrating Halloween, then Thanksgiving. And by then, I'd run out of paper. And it was just me who needed it. There were no signs, sales, hoopla to remind the world at large and my parents in particular that kids need school supplies, not just in September, but all the time.

I learned to lie, to say I was out of paper when I was only running low. And Mom would say, "Okay, I'll get some," then forget. Then I'd run out and have to borrow from my classmates (kids called it "begging"), which was humiliating. So I'd remind her again, and she'd promise to buy some, but forget. Every day the pressure grew, classmates getting increasingly impatient at school, Mom ready to blow at home. And both places I was the beggar. Finally, when it got so bad at school I couldn't stand it, I would walk home, plant my feet and say I REALLY REALLY REALLY need paper. Then she'd get mad. "All right! My goodness! You don't have to make such a fuss!" But, of course, I did. If a teacher had called about the problem, there would have been even bigger trouble.

Maybe God was like that, ready to blow at one request too many. Maybe it was safer just to sit in the back row, scooch down, look at the floor and never raise your hand, even if you really, really had to go. But part of me thought I wasn't just a nuisance and didn't really want to disappear. Maybe it was the voice of the Holy Spirit or my own survival instinct. Or maybe it came through my friends and their parents who liked me and thought I was funny.

. . . . . .

In their company I was good to have around, welcome, not at all a nuisance. Not a beggar. And this impression allowed me to even get irritated sometimes, but only inside.

Since any place was better than home, I loved school and after-school activities, Brownies, then Girl Scouts. I played outdoors or rode my bike until the streetlights came on, my signal to come home. The outdoors smelled so good, sweet and dewy in the morning and, later, of burning leaves and someone's barbecue. Indoors smelled of scorch, something good gone wrong. There were so many rules: family rules and church rules, some spoken, most not. You didn't know you were in trouble until you'd gone "too far," crossed some invisible line that kept changing with the phases of the moon or someone's hormone levels.

Once at church I helped a woman who was a nurse clean and bandage a little child's skinned knee. She said I was a good helper. "You'd make a good nurse some day!" (Nurse and teacher were the two things it was okay for a girl to aspire to). It was a jolt, somebody picturing me in a profession, an adult with a real job. It was probably that small, off-hand remark that made me later, in high school, stick with Latin even though I hated it.

All the essentials were present and accounted for—food, clothes, and shelter. These things are provided even in a home where children are an afterthought, the glue to hold together a wobbly marriage, or a ticket to normalcy, respectability. Man, woman, children, bingo! A family! See? Look at us! Over here! It was the small individual needs and idiosyncrasies that were too much for this boat to float.

So I was grateful for the times when society said to pay attention, the church or calendar or Kresge's windows saying it's time for this or that: school supplies, Trick or Treat, Christmas presents, an Easter bonnet. That would usually mean me too, since other people said so. But on what the Episcopal Church calls "ordinary days," no special time, just everyday life, stay-at-home days, the pull, the clout, all disappeared. I disappeared. On my own, I was on my own.

. . . . . .

Low Profile

BEING INVISIBLE was fairly easy on weekdays. Weekends were a different matter.

Saturday mornings, my Grandpa Keiffer came over. His wife, Julia, my step-grandmother, worked until noon at the bank, so he'd drop her off and come over to our house just to pass the time and find fault. I'd come downstairs in my rumpled pajamas, and he'd say, "Nice outfit!" Or, "That a new hair-do?" Coming from my other grandpa, these remarks would have elicited giggles, but not this one.

So Saturdays, besides avoiding my grandpa, were for chores, homework, washing my hair and listening to Archie on the radio. My dad was home from work, and some chronic tension would be brewing, so if I ran out of things to do in my room, it was a good idea to go to the library or out to play.

But Sundays, everything hit the fan. It was family day, church day. No work, school or shopping (libraries were all closed back then), no errands. No playing outside. No escape. It was a narrow day.

My mom only noticed me when someone else was going to, and Sunday was Looking Day. I was scrubbed, braided and starched. Sunday morning air was acrid with shoe polish, ironing scorch and scolding. We ran around replacing a broken shoelace or a missing button, gathering dusty Bibles that hadn't been touched since last Sunday. Were our Sunday school lessons done for a change? No, we'd have to do them in the car again, on our laps. Quickly. It was only ten blocks to church.

We had Sunday school in a damp basement, the drone of bored teachers reading out of quarterlies and the King James Version of the Bible. They'd take attendance, marking so carefully in that black book with that inky fountain pen, as though a check mark meant you were actually here. If we weren't exactly present, we were certainly accounted for.

· · · · · ·

Once, when I was still very little, I walked by another classroom on my way to the restroom. I overheard a riveting storyteller, her voice full of life and sparkle. I stopped and listened, transfixed. I peeked in to see her putting figures on a flannel-graph board. It was my mother! I'd never heard this voice before, telling exciting adventures of loaves and fishes, arks and rainbows. Was this just for church? Or maybe reserved for when there are lots of kids? And these kids were older than me, school kids. They laughed and raised their hands with the answers, so smart.

Church services were endless. You could either play with the funeral home fans or leaf through the Bible and look at maps of the Holy Land.

Sunday dinner was usually at Grandpa Keiffer's, eating pot roast and gravy and Jell-O salad off round china plates instead of square Malmac, the plastic that lasts forever. Then we kids had to keep quiet if the Cleveland Indians were on the radio. The women talked in the kitchen, and husbands hid behind Sunday newspapers.

A large, ornate golden clock under a glass dome sat on the mantel. Instead of a pendulum, an old-fashioned man and woman in high wigs and fancy dress, did the minuet, round and round, in and out, even though we didn't believe in dancing.

On Sundays, the clock went tick...tock...tick...tock.

Escape to Higher Ground

IT WAS SURPRISINGLY EASY to pack my jammies and get away from home. I just asked, and they said okay and didn't seem to care how long I stayed.

In junior high, I spent sunny, carefree summers at Kathy's parents' summer "cottage" on Sandusky Bay. It was a trailer with a screened-in porch and an outhouse. It was bliss. Her folks smoked, and I remember the smell of smoke waking me up in the mornings. I loved that smell. It meant I was safe, not-home. We'd get up late, go swimming, take out the boat, read comic books, wash the dishes, do our nails, work on our tans and once caught a fish. In the evenings, everyone—kids, adults, neighbors—would gather on the big screened porch, tune into a baseball game or the *Hit Parade* and play Canasta for match sticks.

We never played cards at home, so I learned to deal one-handed on that porch with my right arm in a plaster cast. At first I felt guilty about missing church on Sundays (they were Catholic, so never went to church), but I soon forgot which day of the week it was. I also figured it was because they were Catholic that we had so much freedom, the days light and easy, the nights fun and convivial.

Then one Sunday night in high school, I went home with a church friend for the night and ended up spending the whole summer. And found the same good times even though they were Baptists. Nancy lived in Avon Lake, and it was 1954, the summer that Dr. Sam Shepherd (*The Fugitive*) killed his wife. Of course Nancy didn't live near him. Her dad was a milkman. Dr. Shepherd lived right on the lake in a ranch house with a boat and pier out back. We would look closely at his house when we delivered his paper, and once even paddled our inner tubes over to his pier from the public beach, looking for clues the police might have missed. Now, decades later, it turns out he was innocent. What made us so sure he was guilty? It came out at the trial that he had a girlfriend. Who ever heard of a married man having a *girlfriend*? Of course he was guilty!

Staying with Nancy, I realized that some Christians who attended our church didn't go by all the rules, didn't live cramped, regulated lives with all the keeping track. They were in and out of neighbors' houses, played cards, joined the community band, which played in the square while people danced. I envied this family, committed Christians, active in church, who still went full swing into their little town's social life, taking their place, taking for granted they could do both the secular and sacred without any conflict of interest.

During the school year, as I grew older and had more options, I moved up from baby-sitting to after-school jobs clerking in a store. And I spent the rest of my time swimming at the "Y" or reading at the library, one author leading to another. Finally the head librarian hired me as an assistant, a "page," taught me how to repair book bindings, and I got to stay late and lock up.

What is the opposite of homesickness? A deep longing to get away from home, to get to a different place where love is the bedrock and your place secure. When I was little and still went through the ritual of kissing my parents good night, I often felt a surge of affection for one or the other. I'd hug that one extra hard and just go through the motions with the other. Somehow I could never feel intense love for both of them at the same time so I went to bed feeling vaguely guilty. I wanted to love them both and have them love me and each other, but they were pulling in opposite directions and, if I held on, I would break. It was as if my heart went on strike.

We never jelled as a family, we had no core, no center. Instead we slid around each other like magnets with opposite poles. We could fool others, but not ourselves. Once my mom was featured in the local newspaper as "Homemaker of the Week." She was pictured with one of the afghans she'd made, and the article said she played the organ at church and was president of the PTA. She was quoted as saying, "I want all my children's friends to always feel welcome in our home." I don't know whether they did or not. I know I didn't.

· · · · · ·

The Popsicle Family

OUR NEIGHBORHOOD WENT: street, alley, street, alley. The houses were close together, without driveways, and people parked in the garage out back, off the alley. Our house was so close to our next door neighbors' that we attached hooks to each of our houses and put up a badminton net.

The streets were paved and tree-lined, front lawns green and tidy. The back yards were for garbage cans, swings, hanging laundry and growing tomatoes and rhubarb. Once a week, the garbage trucks rumbled down the black-tarred alley, splashing in the potholes.

In the alley behind our house, some neighbors turned their double garage into a Popsicle factory supplying a local dairy. Nearly every day of summer vacation, Barbara Becker and I each finagled a nickel to buy direct from the manufacturer, little bargain hunters cutting out the middleman, the guy with the white truck who charged a dime. We debated a lot about flavors, but in the end, I always chose cherry, and she always chose orange. When we only had one nickel, the person who paid chose, and we broke it in two. If they were out of cherry or orange, our mutual second choice was grape. On hot, endless summers days, we savored the sweet treat as long as possible, sucking the wooden sticks until we risked tongue splinters, and then we saved the sticks for a doll house we never got around to building.

The Popsicle family was Polish, and theirs was a noisy household. As they worked, they smoked and played loud music or the Cleveland Indians on their radio, fans rotating, mama calling from the house to say someone's wanted on the phone. The guys laughed a lot and wore undershirts that showed their tattoos and tan shoulders.

Sometimes, lying in bed at night, my head on the windowsill, I looked up at the stars through the screen. It was quiet in the neighborhood, but I could hear the Popsicle freezer units hum and click on and off. I'd roll over and look at their house, lit up at night and I'd become Nancy Drew without binoculars, spying on another world, so close and yet so far away. I wondered what it would be like to live in that house, to be a member of that large, loud family, people who talk, have ideas, dreams. I pictured the process of starting out—drawing up a plan at the kitchen table, buying equipment and going into business together, taking a chance, going out on a limb. If it works, great. If not, well, we'll try something else.

I wondered what it would be like to be a part of that family and have the whole wide world to explore, spar with, enjoy. To take some wafer, go to confession and be okay. Or to just be a Presbyterian minding my own business, singing polite hymns and praying in unison from the bulletin. How would it feel to choose from a huge limitless pool for my friends, not just from our little beige church, to be one of the guys instead of one of the chosen few, the salt of the earth: to fall in love once or several times without thought of equal yoking? What would it feel like to be that free, to belong to the community at large? To have no agenda but to live life, bearing no burden for lost souls, having no Great Commission to witness, with no cross to take up daily?

And what would it be like to be Polish-American or Irish-American, Catholic, Jewish, anything except just a regular American with no ethnic background, no connection to anything bigger than this place, this place? We could have a Wednesday night poker game or bridge club instead of Prayer Meeting. We could watch Ed Sullivan on Sunday nights, sleep in Sunday mornings and read the funnies. Why would God make everything so different and wide and wonderful and then say, "No," and point to a narrow path?

If I lived just across the alley, every Friday night I'd walk to the Fish Fry at the Polish-American Club, dance the polka, drink a beer.

What would it be like to live in that house, work in that garage, the smell of ammonia, the grit of sugar underfoot, your hands all the colors of the rainbow?

. . . . .

The Remnant

WHEN YOU'RE LITTLE, it feels cozy and safe to be part of a tight bunch, especially when you're right and everyone else is wrong, like having the Trinity as your peer group. In my world outsiders ranged from the sincere but mistaken to the, let's face it, hell-bound. So if your mom uses Crisco and the neighbor uses Spry, somehow Crisco is the Christian lard.

I went to public school and played with neighbor kids, so I wasn't completely sheltered, but home base was Baptist, and I always had my guard up. We were Christians, but realized that it was a generic term, easily misunderstood and/or preempted by the merely religious, those who were Christians just because they weren't Jewish. Folks around me had a way of saying the word, "*Chrissstian,*" as if it were in italics. "But is he/she a *Chrissstian?*" "Well, it's because I'm a *Chrissstian!*" To be clearer, absolutely certain, we could up the ante to *born-again Chrissstian.* Upon meeting a stranger, we played a little game of who's who. I remember a great aunt coming over to report on a new neighbor. "I saw *two* Bibles." A good sign, but the jury was still out. Once we were sure that someone was a *Chrissstian,* we could relax and enjoy them and gossip. If not, we had to be good witnesses, on our best behavior and always ready to give a word of testimony or at least invite them to church.

But if the cornerstone of your faith is the literal interpretation of an inerrant Bible, you get very good at beady-eyed scrutiny and eventually find something, even among born-again *Chrissstians,* to disagree on. And you can't let bygones be bygones, just agree to disagree, because that way lies compromise (bad word), the slippery slope that leads to liberalism. You must, in good conscience, dig in your heels. "For what fellowship hath righteousness with unrighteousness?" "Can two walk together unless they be agreed?"

We went to the First Baptist Church until I was about ten and then went with a splinter group over some small but vital point of doctrine. Our group, the true remnant of believers, founded the Church of the Open Door, which was always locked. I overheard a woman tell someone, when questioned about our former affiliation with the Baptists, "It's like cream rises to the top." Our move away from the denomination was a natural process of purification.

After our move, if questioned about my religious affiliation (which almost never happens to a ten-year-old) I could no longer answer, "Baptist." Suddenly I wasn't only different from non-believers, but from all denominations and their larger context. I would never go from our little cement block church to a large Baptist camp or the state conference of Young Lutherans. When traveling, we couldn't just pop into any old church for worship and fellowship. We were, like our church, independent, unaffiliated, accountable only the Lord with the Bible as our "only rule for faith and practice." When asked what religion I was, I was to say, "I'm a *Chrissstian!*"

When someone asked what kind of church the Church of the Open Door was, we were warned against saying interdenominational, which was (bad word) inclusive and sounded embracing and all-encompassing, something we certainly were not. We were to say instead, "nondenominational." Denominations were part of (more bad words) "organized religion." Could my little ten-year-old brain keep these two long words straight? Our favorite Scripture was, "Come out from among them and be ye separate," better than, surer than, holier than, not just thou, but everyone, even other Baptists.

We sang, "Shall the Circle be Unbroken?" I couldn't answer that, but our circle sure kept shrinking.

The Second Coming

There is laid up for me a crown of righteousness... and not for me only,
but for all who love his appearing.
—2 Timothy 4:8

THE SUNDAY SCHOOL TEACHER leans forward and asks us sixth graders, "Do you love his appearing? Jesus is coming back. It's a good test of your faith: how much do you look forward to the Second Coming?"

Well, to tell the truth, not at all. I haven't even menstruated yet. I know we believers live in the hope of his resurrection and coming again. I know the songs and Scriptures and adults who say so. And, in the early fifties, with the A-bomb tests, with Civil Defense alarms interrupting geography class, the end times are very real to me. Joseph McCarthy is on our tiny, new, black-and-white television, exposing Communists at high levels of government. Aha! Just last Saturday, my brother broke a record I'd bought with my hoarded allowance. It was a record of the Weavers singing "Weemaweh," and he'd heard they were Communists.

At church on Sunday night, fundamentalist films combine terrifying shots of a mushrooming cloud exploding over the desert, with voice-overs from the Book of Revelation, until we are all petrified and walk the aisle, joining in the pew-emptying responses to long, heart-wrenching altar calls. I'd sure rather go and be with the Lord than be left behind for the Tribulation when all water turns to blood, and blood flows as deep as horses' necks. But most of all, I'd like to make cheerleader.

But the fear was never far away. I was at a pajama party one evening, half of us were in the bathtub, when the power went off, leaving us in pitch-black darkness. The others squealed and giggled, but I reached over to the dripping faucet and tasted the water to see if it had turned to blood. What if the Rapture comes and I'm left behind? Did I not choose to come to this Saturday night sleepover, knowing I'd miss church tomorrow morning? Don't I daydream for hours about romance, or being a country music star, or at least a Red Cross nurse with a crisp white hat and a long navy cape that swoops behind me as I run into the smoking wreckage? How much time do I spend on my knees, praying and yearning for Christ's return?

My Aunt Beulah yearns. Her annual Christmas letters are a litany of woes: who died, who's sick, who's getting divorced. She recounts all the year's natural disasters (fortunately, she lives in California), as signs of the end times. And the last sentence is always the same. "Even so, come quickly, Lord Jesus."

Do I ever feel that way? Maybe, when Betty Jo has a birthday party and invites everyone but me. Maybe when I enter the cafeteria with a tray full of lunch, my usual lunch period changed because of a special orchestra practice, and face a vast roomful of kids settled into their regular places, saving all the empty spots with books and purses and sweaters. "This would be a good time, Lord!"

Sure, it's easy for older people like my aunt, in her thirties, whose life is almost over. But I'm young! I'm just beginning to feel the stirrings of girl-feelings, the joy of good friends, inside jokes, hearing the laughter to the skit I wrote for assembly. I can see the light of college at the end of the dark tunnel that is my parents' marriage. And this, this is when you want me to reject "the World," set my affection on things above, not on things below? Have you seen the new guy in my Algebra class? Okay, we're all mortal. This world is not our home, we're just a-passin' through, but I've just discovered Tangee lipstick. And lemon Cokes. Emily Dickinson! Twirly cheerleader skirts and knee socks and saddle shoes!

So, no, Sunday school teacher, I don't yearn for the end of life as I know it. And don't want to, if it means souring on this world, poking and sniffing and pointing out all the ways life and people fail us, but Jesus never fails. I know I'm supposed to hate the world, but I love it and want to stay until the very end. Or at least until I menstruate.

Section III · Mid-fifties

Teenville

THE CHURCH NEVER PAID much attention to me until I started high school. Compliant children were shuttled around to Sunday school classes, church, Sunday school picnics, prayer meetings. New dress at Easter, children's party at Christmas when we are each given slices of Neapolitan ice cream. Missionaries with their natives-with-goiters slides, reciting John 3:16 in a singsong foreign tongue. All in all, if you were neither very naughty nor "the best," a child could slip along unnoticed at church indefinitely.

But I turned thirteen in the early fifties, shortly after America invented teens. Bam! High schools sponsor Friday night sock hops, "mixers," and proms; stores sell *Seventeen* magazine; Archie and his friends jump off the comic page and come alive every Saturday morning on the radio with squeaky, just-changing voices.

High school celebrities are jocks and cheerleaders. Booted majorettes strut and throw flaming batons at half time. Movies, always a tool of the devil, are being made and marketed just for this new breed—teens. They show teens frolicking on the beach, necking at drive-ins, eating hamburgers at soda shops, racing cars at midnight—more things to pray about at Prayer Meeting.

We said, "I don't believe in dancing," which was pretty silly. I mean there it was from time immemorial. Hebrews danced through the Old Testament, even in the King James Version, glorifying and praising God. Over the whole earth, people danced at weddings and funerals, marking life's milestones. And every single Saturday night in gyms and Ys, ballrooms and the Catholic church basement, nearly every young person in Elyria, Ohio, was at a dance, dancing. Of course we meant we didn't believe Christians should dance.

. . . . . .

When I started high school, my parents told me I was old enough to make my own decisions. I knew what they believed, had heard about the dancing issue in church and Sunday school through junior high, and they trusted me now to decide for myself. The first day of school, they announced over the PA system a freshman "Get-Acquainted Dance," girls to ask boys. I leaned over and asked Alan, our paperboy, a quiet good friend I really liked. He said, "Sure!" That night, when I told my parents, they had a short conference and decided I wasn't old enough after all. "What would people think?" Mom even declared, "It would kill your grandfather," a moot point, since he was already dead.

I called Alan to cancel. How can I explain? Church leaders said the reason for our "stand" was that dancing led to sexual promiscuity. So I lied and told Alan I was sick. I never asked my parents when I *would* be able to make my own decisions. I just kept quiet and played it safe. The only time I had gone out on a limb, I'd ended up deeply embarrassing myself, not to mention the paperboy.

"See You at the 'Y'"

THE NEW "Y" that opened in 1955 was quite a change from the drafty old barn with its cavernous multi-purpose room where as kids we sang camp songs, earned our Girl Scout badges and traded misinformation about sex. The new facility had a Teen Center with a dance floor, soda fountain, and lounge with a fireplace. After school, we girls sat on the floor and did our homework, but it came alive on Friday and Saturday nights. Any time there wasn't a game or school function, the lights went up, the doors flung open, and the 78s and 45s stated spinning. Heaven.

I'd never been allowed to go to school dances, but this was a Teen Center, a place to just hang out with your friends, and I wanted to go. To avoid the dance issue and have a legitimate reason for being there, I volunteered to work at the soda fountain, assisting Martha's mom. We all loved Mrs. Cook, a cheerful, rotund woman with pierced ears, colorful clothes and an easy laugh. I spent all my baby-sitting money on an aqua felt skirt decorated not with poodles, but with a bright red lobster appliqué. Goldfish swam around the hem, and pearls bubbled up from their mouths in a wavy stream. The only type of lipstick I was allowed to wear was Tangee. It added no more hue than Vaseline but made my lips feel waxy and full.

The first thing Mrs. Cook handed me was a hair net and a large white apron, but I was happy just to be there, in the center of the Teen Center, learning the ropes of ice cream soda-making, the double-jolt of chocolate Cokes and, everyone's favorite, chocolate malts. She urged me to take a break, but this was my dream job, being part of things while in no danger of being asked to dance, a princess surrounded by a moat of counter top and swivel stools. When she insisted, I went into the lounge, pretended to look at *Seventeen* magazine and wondered if the Bunny Hop (more a game than a dance) would be okay. But then I'd be out on the dance floor, right? And what would I do if someone asked me to dance? Hand

. . . . . .

him a tract? Start a theological discussion in my stocking feet? I decided on an extended stay in the restroom, freshening my Tangee.

Somewhere along the line, Martha's mom must have noticed my dilemma and spoke to my mom about it. I don't know what she said, but it embarrassed my mom to be put on the spot. My dad reminded me that being a Christian was more than just a fire escape from hell. And I wasn't allowed to go to the Teen Center any more. I guess the deal was that you had to refrain from dancing, plus be happy about it.

I knew a little church history. (For my sixteenth birthday, my grandfather Keiffer gave me Fox's *Book of Martyrs*.) And compared to being burned at the stake for being a Christian, staying home on Friday nights was no big deal. Some of our closest friends were missionaries who told about people banished and even tortured for their faith. We heard, "When in doubt, don't!" Don't what? And doubts? I was plagued with doubts! Am I pretty? Does he like me? Could I dance even if I tried?

If you layer the dark side of religion on top of a natural Midwest reserve, you get a people who don't know how to party even on a modest scale. We could weep with those who wept but didn't have a clue how to rejoice with those who rejoiced. The most we could do when people got a big promotion, graduated, or got married, was say, "Good for you!" or "Praise the Lord!"

At Christmas we shook our heads over the commercialization of a sacred holiday, saw in the Babe of Bethlehem the Christ of Calvary, reminded each other that one of the Wise Men brought embalming fluid as a gift. At weddings, after a sermon about the two becoming one flesh that never mentioned the Wedding Feast at Cana, we trooped into the fellowship hall for a sugar feast of cookies and mints and wedding cake. We didn't even propose a toast to the bride and groom with our Hawaiian punch, because that might look, to outsiders, too much like the world.

. . . . . .

Meanwhile, when a boy did ask me out, it was almost always either to a movie or dance, the two taboos. I couldn't accept but couldn't really explain either. I was too shy to say, "That's against my religion. How about bowling instead?" Most didn't ask again. It didn't occur to most of us in the fifties that a girl could ask a boy out, show her interest with a casual invitation to have an after-school Coke together. And if it had occurred to me, I probably wouldn't have had the courage to do it. So I had lots of friends in high school, but never, ever a boyfriend.

Snow White Gets a Brother

BY THE TIME I WAS FOURTEEN, whatever brinkmanship my parents worked out to keep a split at bay was breaking down. Nobody ever actually used the "d" word. Divorce wasn't an option for born-again Christians. You didn't go to your pastor for help. Pastors were preachers. They delivered sermons and met with the deacons to go over the blueprints for the new Sunday school wing. They had no training in counseling, marriage or otherwise. The only people I ever knew who were divorced were certainly not Christians. They usually hung out at the bus station. Divorce for my parents, just because they didn't get along, was unthinkable. What was the answer for a Christian couple who fought all the time? Pray harder?

My dad was either silent or yelling, as though he'd lost his middle gears. Somehow Mom had misplayed her hand, gone too far, and Dad was moving out. Each night, when the library finally closed and I came home, Dad would be waiting for me in the living room. "You can just tell her that once I leave, I'm not coming back," he'd tell me. "I can get better treatment from strangers. I'd be better off with a room at the 'Y.'" I'd go upstairs to my mom and deliver his latest ultimatum. "Well, you can just tell *him*...."

Finally, one night I told her that it was no use. He was really leaving this time. And I started to cry. She said, "Don't worry, it will work out." And it did.

While he was packing, she dropped her bomb. She was pregnant. So he didn't leave and I, a sophomore in high school, was going to have a little brother or sister. When my best friend asked why my parents were having another baby at this age, I told her because they'd run out of things to fight about.

Mom went into labor on April first. That night I waited up in the living room but fell asleep about three in the morning. My dad called to say the baby was born, a boy. I was groggy, and it was all so surreal. He asked if I'd been asleep, and I lied and said, "No." He said that I certainly didn't sound very happy! This was my brother, after all! Didn't I realize how hard this was on a woman her age? Gethsemane—and I couldn't even stay awake. Then there were "complications," and she was in the hospital a couple of weeks. So I was in charge of the house and my eight-year-old brother.

One of the constant conflicts in our home was housework. My dad wanted a neat and orderly house, and Mom didn't take to housework. In neighborhoods like ours, women didn't work and maids were for rich people. So my mom was a housewife, wore house dresses, listed herself as a "homemaker," but rarely did housework unless company was coming. She was always busy about something, just not cleaning or laundry. She'd start a few chores, chat with neighbors, talk on the phone, go shopping and start a few more chores. So Dad usually came home to dirty dishes, unmade beds and the vacuum cleaner or ironing board in the living room for several days in a row. His only communication with us kids was, "Where's your mom?" Since he couldn't get her to do housework, he tried to enlist me, the oldest and only daughter, and this led to the only time he ever hit me.

My favorite cousin was over. I'd done my chores and wanted to visit with her, so when he told me to clean the kitchen too, I objected. He hit me so hard he nearly knocked me over, and my mouth bled. I couldn't believe it. I went to my room crying, and later my mom came up and told me I should be ashamed of myself. "Your dad is down there with tears in his eyes washing the dishes."

With Mom in the hospital, it was all up to me. And I had no idea where to begin. It was 1952, and *Snow White*, Disney's first full-length animation, was at the theaters. I'd never seen it, of course, but I knew the songs by heart. One went, "This is the way we wash our clothes, early Monday morning." Tuesdays were for ironing, Wednesdays baking, Thursdays cleaning, and so on. I decided to give it a try. I set my alarm for early Monday morning and did the

. . . . . .

laundry, hung it out on the line before school, took it down when I got home, folded and put away most of it, sprinkled the ironing for the next morning. That wasn't so hard. No more "mystery chute," where things disappeared for weeks or months. Each day I also straightened the house, made the beds, swept or vacuumed and did dishes after each meal. It only took an hour or so and the house looked great. I was proud to invite friends home.

By the time my mom got home from the hospital, I was really mad at her. Basic housework wasn't hard at all. I vowed in my heart never to live in an untidy house. Nobody in my house would ever have to paw through the hamper for yesterday's socks. I'd have a house that was pretty and neat, with good smells from baking, music playing and flowers from the garden.

I've lived in many places since then, in many different circumstances. With working full-time, it often would have made more sense to do laundry on weekends, but it's always done on Mondays as a promise to that little girl. For the most part, the two of us enjoy a clean house with good smells and flowers. That short period of keeping house showed me I could have an impact on my environment. I could and would choose a different way to live.

Testimonies

Belonging to an ultra-conservative church meant attending church often and limiting our social life to other Christians, so we didn't have may close relationships with unbelievers. We weren't very involved with our neighbors or office colleagues and didn't belong to any fraternal or social or even charity organizations, letting the dead bury their dead, like Jesus told his disciples. So, when it came to witnessing, we practiced on each other. And we had plenty of practice. Our services were full of testimonies. Sunday morning testimonies were called for whenever there was a pause, maybe while someone came up from the back to give an announcement or while the special music tuned up. "Anyone got a word of testimony?"

Even though an unsaved person would be more likely to visit on Sunday morning, most testimonies were saved for Sunday evenings, called Evangelistic Services. Compared to the rest of the service, a call for testimonies was sort of exciting because you never knew what would happen next. What if no one stood up? That would be an occasion for shame. "What? Nobody has a word for the Lord?" What if two people stood up at once? What if you stood up and drew a blank?

Since most members had been Christians all their lives, we didn't hear about recent conversions but about having too little faith along the Christian walk. "I was in this situation and it looked bad, but then the Lord came through. Why didn't I have more faith?" Or someone would quote a favorite verse of Scripture or a part of a hymn. Some had direct revelations. "I was praying and the Lord told me...." But one thing was always sure: Miss Preston in her navy hat—straw in summer, wool in winter—would stand and say: "Jesus Christ—the same yesterday, today and forever." And everyone would say "A-men." Year in, year out, she said this same thing any time testimonies were called for.

. . . . . .

And Miss Preston's testimony fit in with what we believed, underlined it. While the world was searching for truth, madly flailing around for some satisfaction and wisdom, we had the Answer. And he/it never changed. People read and traveled far and wide, searched the world over and then re-searched. But not us. Our old-time religion was good enough for mother, and it's good enough for us. We didn't even need the latest version of the Bible. If the King James Bible was good enough for Paul, it was good enough for us.

But it was the degree of certainty that made me somehow even less sure of what I believed. "Others say they *hope* they're going to heaven. I'm glad I *know!*" "Some say they think they're saved, but I'm 100 percent certain!" "My neighbor went to a fortune teller. But I believe like the song says, 'I know not what the future holds, but I know who holds the future.'" A-men.

Well, I know the Lord holds the future too. But I'm scared anyway. This is the fifties: bomb shelters, air raids and the Red Menace. I'm scared of the Communists *and* the Second Coming. And I'm not 100 percent sure of anything. I don't fit in with those regular, free, worldly people home watching Ed Sullivan or these glowing, visionary Christians with a direct pipeline to God. Pretty soon the announcements are done, the violin is tuned and testimonies are over. And the next hymn is "That Old-time Religion."

Why does this irritate me so? These are good people. They were my Sunday school and Daily Vacation Bible School teachers when I had pigtails. They taught me the books of the Bible with a game called "Sword Drill," taught me the lifelong lesson that the Bible is a daily guide, an openable book. They gave me my perfect attendance pin, each new year dangling under the last one. They put gold stars on my chart when I recited my Memory Verse by heart. They love the Lord and want the best for me. What makes me want to scream?

. . . . . .

Well, for one thing, the phrase, "good enough." It's so brain-shutting-down, so set in stone. Settle down, young lady. Settle for what you've got, what's here, all spelled out. I know you might think you want that, but you'd better settle for this. It may not be the best, but it's good enough. Who do you think you are anyway?

I can look at nature and see there is order to the universe, a Creator. I know some things never change, but I haven't decided what they are yet. That's why I read Tournier and Bonhoeffer and Weatherhead under the covers at night while my friends read *Winds of War* by Herman Wouk, especially the parts about sex. In *Living Together,* Dietrich Bonhoeffer says Christian fellowship is to be rare and serendipitous. Besides periodic corporate worship, we are to be out there, in and among others, believers and unbelievers alike. How does this fit in with a Christian bowling league?

So please don't tell me to "settle." I want to experiment, learn, wonder, grow, go places. I've got questions. I've got doubts. I've got my whole life ahead of me. I've got a library card!

After Evangelistic Service we go to Young People's. The pianist is late, so the leader calls for testimonies. I stand up and say, "My testimony, the same yesterday, today and forever." My friends laugh, but I know that I'll never be president of Young People's now.

Walking the Walk

BESIDES WITNESSING, EVANGELIZING, and inviting people to church, we were to live our faith. The obvious priority was attending church, even on trips. "Don't take a vacation from God." And attending church wasn't because you had to, but because you wanted to. "I was glad when they said to me, let us go unto the house of the Lord." People who go Sunday mornings love the church, Sunday evenings, love the people, Wednesday nights, love the Lord. So here's the scale. Add up the amount of time you spend at church, and we can see your commitment to the Lord.

During spring and fall, revival services were held every night for a week. One Friday night, I was with my (secular) friends at a drive-in restaurant near the church after a football game. It was Fall Revival and the church parking lot was packed. I hoped nobody would notice, but someone did. "Look Barb! There's something going on at your church. How come you're not there?" "Oh," I lied, "it's special meetings all week long, but they're all the same and I went last night."

Besides attending church, we were to abstain from evil and *all appearances of evil*. The implications of "appearances of evil" were pernicious, like an ink stain seeping into linen. Meeting a friend downtown to shop for new shoes, and she asks you to meet her outside the movie theater? Wouldn't just standing out there look like you were going in? What if a weaker Christian were to drive by and see you and misunderstand, be tempted into sin? Better meet in front of the hardware store.

Of course, if your friend had been at the movies, you'd better think twice about hanging around with her at all. Besides church attendance and avoiding all appearances of evil, your choice of friends should be confined to true, evangelical Christians, "in honor preferring one another."

· · · · · ·

A wholehearted commitment to Christ naturally influenced your future as an adult: Christian college, Christian mate (be not unequally yoked together with unbelievers), type of career, the top being "full-time Christian service," such as marrying a minister. Even lay vocations were not just jobs, but ministries: chances to witness to those in the business community. "Our new son-in-law has been called to the parking lot attendant ministry." Girls who weren't married by twenty could feel the call to full-time Christian service as a missionary, as long as you went far enough away.

In my senior year, the high school held a series of weekly panel discussions on different aspects of adult life—college, career, money management. (This was the fifties, so sex wasn't something adults discussed in public. On television married couples had twin beds, but Lucy managed to get pregnant anyway.) One of these sessions was on religion, and there were four panelists—a Protestant, a Catholic, a Jew and me. They knew I was *something.* I suppose I should have felt honored, but I just felt embarrassed. I don't remember much about the evening, but I do recall reluctantly answering questions about Jewish traditions and holidays because Dick Klein didn't actually know anything about being a Jew. Or maybe he just wanted to distance himself from being different too.

So we had Christian films, Christian colleges, bookstores, yellow pages, a whole subculture of ways to come out from among them and be separate. But it seemed to me like a pale imitation of the secular and sometimes just felt clannish. Did being a Christian really mean you had to decorate with Hummel figures and have all your car radio buttons tuned to Christian stations? Did loving the Lord mean abstaining from all the performing arts except for organ music, Andy Williams and Billy Graham films?

Way before the Moral Majority, being a Christian influenced how you voted. Who would make the best president, senator, mayor? Who was a Christian? Somehow in 1980, we got mixed up and backed the divorced movie star instead of the born-again Baptist Sunday school teacher.

. . . . . .

In Sunday school and Young People's, we were urged, as we approached adulthood, to seek God's will for our lives. God's will for my dad had been to be a missionary, but my mom had a lot of medical problems (we didn't have insurance but were supposed to trust the Lord), and they came home to earn money to pay off the bills. Then they bought a house, and it became apparent that my dad wasn't going back. What happened to his "call," his ordination into the ministry? He explained that serving as a layman in church was God's "secondary" will for him, the primary having been the ministry, which didn't work out. Of course, he never told me this directly. I just happened to be in a Sunday school class he was teaching on the subject of "God's will."

When tragedy struck and we wondered how God could let this happen, it was God's "passive" will. He didn't want it to happen but had obviously let it happen, maybe to teach us a lesson such as how fleeting life was. When someone was healed or saved, it was God's "active" will. The pinnacle was to be in the center of God's "perfect" will, the divine equivalent of a bull's eye.

So while my classmates were applying for college admissions and scholarships, anxiously watching the mail, taking vocational tests and meeting with guidance counselors, I was to pray to find this one narrow magic path that made all the difference. It felt like a riddle to be solved, as if God were clutching this single, solitary, blessed plan for my life to his bosom, and it was my job to ferret out the right answer. We had God's will—primary and secondary, active and passive. And perfect.

The envelope, please.

. . . . . .

Hi-B.A.

High School Born-Againers

IN RESPONSE TO THE LURE of the world, the flesh and the devil, the church hired a youth director, budgeted money for a youth program and scheduled something whenever there was a dance at the high school to offer a wholesome alternative, such as bowling or roller-skating. Or hay rides. That's it, a hay ride! Nature, rural setting, All-American farm, take their minds off sex. Let them lie under blankets, on soft mounds of sweet-smelling hay, on a gently swaying wagon and look up at the stars in heaven that God made. They'll never even think about sex! Put on a Spring Banquet the same night as the prom, a special night: formals, dates, corsages. Spaghetti in the Fellowship Hall should do it if we put up enough crepe paper. For entertainment, we'll rent a Moody Science Film on the evils of evolution. We could probably even get the pastor himself to be the after-dinner speaker.

I had the lead in my senior class play and came off it high. (Although we never attended movies or live theatre, school plays, like the orchestra and band, were a part of our education, and all the drama teacher's choices wholesome). The boyfriend my folks favored, Jerry, drove me home after the last curtain call. Of course I couldn't go to the cast party. There might be dancing. I told him I thought I'd like to go into drama. I thought no such thing but wanted to wriggle out of any future with him and a Christian college. (This was before my pastor informed me that Bob Jones University had a drama major.) We could hardly be meant for each other if God was calling me to Hollywood and Jerry to serve God by taking over his dad's Ford dealership. Jerry reluctantly admitted that there was certainly a need for Christian movies, taking for granted I'd meant acting in Billy Graham films. My folks kept asking what was wrong with him, as though I had to come up with a reason for not marrying someone who looked perfectly fine to them.

. . . . . .

If I felt isolated at school, I felt even more isolated at church where the pressure was on. They didn't just want me to believe for myself (which I did), but to witness, to proclaim the gospel to others (which I didn't). I was to have a vision of my high school as a mission field, pass out tracts in the halls, carry my Bible on top of my books. When someone asked, "Why are you carrying a Bible?" it would be a fine chance to witness, to say, "Because it's the road map to heaven!" Poor kid. He was just looking for the cafeteria.

High School Born-Againers met every Monday night. The leader came from Cleveland to teach us how to evangelize our high school. How else would they hear about the gospel, we were asked, as if we lived in Botswana. How would they be saved if we didn't go forth to win them? Instead of going forth, I preferred to just crawl into my locker.

Any reluctance to witness was labeled disloyalty to the Lord. In Romans it says that if we are ashamed of Christ, he will be ashamed of us. The thought of Jesus hanging his head, being ashamed of me, turning away in eternity, was unbearable. But I would rather eat glass than hand someone a tract. Maybe I could just leave them on the backs of the toilets in the girls' restroom.

Every Monday night we got a new handout, some trinket or printed matter, a "wedge of witness." And we were to report the next Monday how it had been used. The tracts had the plan of salvation and our church name rubber-stamped on the back. Pencils were printed with FGSLTWTHGHOBSTWBINSNPBHEL (Jn 3:16). We were given pins to wear with just a question mark. When someone asked about it, you said, "If you were to die today, would you go to heaven?" This clearly is not the way to get elected class secretary or even get a date, but what was more important, saving souls or being popular? And we were the "only Bible some people would ever read."

We were coached in what to say in science class when evolution was taught, how to refute an English teacher who refers to the Bible as simply great literature, what to do in phys ed when square dancing was today's exercise. And pressure was greatest on seniors. We heard about some kids who went to school together all their lives and then, on graduation, one bunch went out drinking and all died in a car crash, unsaved and doomed for eternity, because the one Christian around them had never witnessed. These were people we would probably never see again, and there were only months, then weeks, then days left for us to make an everlasting difference in their lives.

• • •

It's June 1956, the night of graduation. This whole year I've heard how important it is to witness to my classmates, my last chance. And still I didn't evangelize, didn't speak out, didn't even glow so much that people came to me to ask what it was about me that was different.

My closest friends are Honor Society Methodists and the others, the wild ones, Catholic. But no one from either group is born-again after years of hanging around with me. And now it is too late. Four years of failure, so much shame. So I cry myself to sleep.

Section IV • Late Fifties

The Gift

I AM SIXTEEN and in a motel room in Greenville, South Carolina, with my parents and brothers. Tomorrow they drive back home, and I start college. I'd love to spend this night in my shiny, new dorm room in my cozy bottom bunk with the new flowered sheets, a graduation present. I've already laughed with my wonderful new roommate and the campus is so clean and orderly: happy reunions, orientations, the smell of biscuits and chicory coffee for breakfast. I feel the bubble rising within me. I imagine I'll soon be free of the crusty cocoon of my parents' pain for good. One night on a motel rollaway bed, a small price to pay. One more night to keep up the pretense of family.

But some awful, familiar conflict is in the air, over what? Anything, nothing, something. All is misery. I am mad that they can't be civil to each other for one night for my sake. Yet I feel bad that I'm leaving them behind, to their own devices, taking away their buffer, the Bufferin that somewhat, sometimes, dulls the symptoms but never even dents the true source of pain. The next morning my dad offers an indirect apology. "Sorry about that," and I blurt out, "Maybe it will be better without me." He says, "No, this isn't your fault. We're not a regular family, not like a family should be." The dam that is my mother breaks. How can he say such a thing? All families have problems! Nobody's perfect! She's madder than I've ever seen her. Her fury scares me. Does admitting the truth, even to a daughter, ruin everything?

But I feel grateful. I can't ever remember his going out on a limb for me before or since. For now he's let me off the hook of blame, let me know I'm not crazy. And he will pay for a long time. Oh, will he pay.

Later my aunts tell me that after I left, my dad just gave up. But I think he'd given up long before that.

. . . . . .

Campus Life

IT WAS A GREAT RELIEF to be at Bob Jones University. Everyone was saved, so nobody would go to hell because I failed to witness. The Bible was central to every rule, class lecture and chapel service, so I was no longer "the only Bible some people would ever read." I was only sixteen but already tired of being urged to fight the powers of darkness, the world, the flesh and the devil, in the form of movies, proms and pancake makeup. Here I didn't have to fight any more. Here these worldly activities were stopped at the gate: why the barbed wire slanted out. Now I could jump in with both feet socially and academically. No dancing or Darwin.

Days were as orderly as a convent: morning devotions, breakfast, classes, chapel, lunch and more classes. After dinner was Mission Prayer Band, where we gathered in different sections of the chapel according to the country we had the most interest in. Groups were often led by "MKs," missionaries' kids, and included specific prayer requests and the latest news from each mission field. We felt a real bond with those we prayed for when we knelt next to one of their daughters. Up front a map of the world had tiny light bulbs wherever Bob Jones graduates served. Where is God calling you?

Then there were wonderful evenings in the dorms, where portable typewriters clicked and people knocked softly before entering your room. The day ended with ten o'clock prayers, four rooms to a prayer group. It was okay to come in your jammies. Eleven o'clock was lights out, seven days a week. On weekends hair dryers whirred, starched crinolines dried on open umbrellas, and the air was full of the smell of shampoo, floor wax and popcorn. The only dating was on campus, at school-sponsored activities such as concerts or banquets. Or you could meet a date at the "Furniture Store," the school's official dating parlor, above the Student Center, a sea of sofas, and spend the evening talking and flirting at least six inches apart. This life was so peaceful and clean, the opposite of the chaos at home. Here all the rules were posted on the back of each dorm room door, and standards for behavior were clear. Griping was not tolerated. The discipline committee met every Saturday morning, but I was used to following rules and never had to go.

I loved my roommate, my teachers and new friends. I could accept dates and receive corsages, fall in love, even, without fear of being "unequally yoked." I could finally wear formals, although they had to pass inspection. My mom had made me a taffeta formal and it was deemed doubtful by the Dean of Women when she saw it on the hanger. But when I tried it on, it passed. Back in my room I stood in front of the mirror, lifted my arms and turned around, trying to find how it might be immodest. What did they know that I didn't?

Besides dorm life, the best part of college was studying without distraction in the library or dorm study halls. Science classes, taught by a married couple who were both recent BJU graduates, were laced with theology about God's wonders. We memorized a list of the many flaws in the secular humanist research that had come up with the laughable theory of evolution. In art classes, we painted clothed figures and learned crafts for Daily Vacation Bible School. One psychology professor said to ignore your dreams because they were "garbage." There was just the one introductory psych course, because offering a psychology major attracted the wrong types.

Only boys could study for the ministry, but girls could major in Christian education and take free piano lessons. In speech class we were given a list of poems and recitations to choose from for class oration. Anything not on the list had to be approved beforehand. All text and library books had notices glued in the flyleaf to the effect that the contents of this book are not necessarily approved by the University. "...it is sometimes necessary to use textbooks whose contents the University cannot wholly endorse. You understand, of course, that acceptable textbooks in certain academic fields are very difficult to secure."

. . . . . .

During the first week of classes, I was in English class where the teacher told us about an amazing thing—the *Oxford English Dictionary*. You could follow the history of any word all the way back, for me a dream come true. I tuned out the rest of the lecture and began a letter to my parents. It was September. If I started my campaign now and continued unabated for three months, maybe I would prevail. "This is what I want for Christmas, all I want for Christmas. I don't care what condition it's in. If it's falling apart, I'll put it back together with duct tape. And I'll never ask for anything else again in my whole life. Please, please, please." After class I mailed the letter and headed straight to the library. I asked the librarian where the *Oxford English Dictionary* was, and she pointed to a shelf of books. Which one is it? "All of them." My college education had begun.

Religious Education

DR. BOB JONES, SR. was the founder of the school, and one of his favorite sayings was, "There is no difference between the secular and the sacred; to the Christian all things are sacred." And this was borne out in life on campus. There were official times and places for religious education and worship, such as morning chapel and Sunday services. And classes all had a strong religious component with one of the founder's sayings posted above each blackboard. But spiritual matters pervaded every phase of our life together from private conversations to the student handbook.

Meals, with assigned seats, started with grace and one faculty or staff member hosted each table, usually just chatting, but ready to monitor and censure our conversation if necessary. You learned quickly which faculty members would be good company and tried to casually choose a seat as far away from the others as possible. Morning devotions, chapel, Mission Prayer Band and evening prayers—the day was saturated with religious faith and practice.

Of course chapel was required. It was held every morning at ten-thirty, starting promptly, as did all classes and meals, with military precision. Bell, hymn, offering, prayer, announcements, sermon, hymn, bell, out. The militant fervor prevailed even in the hymns, favorites being "Onward, Christian Soldiers," and "Who Is on the Lord's Side?" We were soldiers of the cross in basic training, victorious over sin, winning the battle, armed with the Sword of the Lord, eyes on the prize, faithful, loyal, true. (The school radio station was called Tower of Power and broadcast gospel messages and music all day long, WMUU-AM, World's Most Unusual University, on the far right of your dial). Chapel speakers were usually one of the three Dr. Bobs, a faculty member, or BJU graduate—all male, of course.

Within a few weeks we knew the drill: give your heart, your life, your all. Gird your loins. Here come the Preacher Boys (those studying for the ministry), sitting up front together in chapel, the stars, the front-line soldiers, the elite, the truly committed ones. Every weekend they're sent in teams or pairs to preach the gospel on street corners or in small churches.

On Saturday mornings, we girls carried flannel-graph boards to Milltown, barren acres of shacks for hundreds of mill workers. We did puppet shows and gave out treats from our own allowances. We were a big hit. There wasn't much to do Saturday mornings in Milltown.

The Preacher Boys' standing assignment for any school break was to witness to at least one person a day and submit a written account. Completing this assignment was necessary for graduation. But summer is a long time, which leads to fudging. Asked to say grace at a family reunion? Throw in the plan of salvation, some Scripture and give yourself the month of July off! Say grace with friends before lunch in a restaurant? Give yourself credit for ten days. Surely that many patrons noticed your "witness."

Sunday school classes on campus were by denomination and are theoretically voluntary, but attendance is taken. If you missed two Sundays in a row, the Dean of Religion called you in for a talk. Sunday services were open to the public, and girls wore hats and gloves.

But chapel was just for us students, and we were often told that the sheltered, controlled environment of this campus was like a greenhouse, ideal for growing sturdy witnesses to go out in the field and sow the gospel, but life in the world will be the real test. Were we ready? Will we be found able to take a stand and never, ever compromise?

There may be a fine line between education and indoctrination, but at chapel the gloves were off. Sermons were fiery and fierce. Witness, win them over! Be the first to spot the enemy! Mow down the devil and his cohorts with the mighty Scripture. Cut off the unbeliever's protests with the "right" answers. Always be ready to give an answer for the faith that lieth in you. Ready? Swords drawn? The Lord needs us, we are his army, heresy-seeking missiles are we! Sinners? Boom! Compromisers? Boom! Liberals? Modernists? Agnostics?

. . . . .

Boom! Christian militia, loners, of course, having come out from among the merely church-goers. It's not an easy road. Everyone's against a true believer. The whole world is going down, down. And the plan of salvation is so simple if only they would listen!

• • •

A decade later I would be a pastor's wife—married a Preacher Boy—when the house near-est to our rural church burned down. Someone asked, "What shall we do?" The reply, "Why should we help? They were out in some bar when it happened." Boom!

Another decade and I'm divorced, an Episcopalian in church with Jan, an old BJ friend. The priest says, "If you'd like to know God's will for your life, I'll tell you." He moves to the right section of the church. "Okay, from this aisle over, here is God's will for you: Be neighborly." He moves to the left. "From this aisle over, here's God's will for *you*: Love your neighbor." Center section: "Love your neighbor." I ask Jan if we ever heard that. "In all our years at Bob Jones, did we ever hear that?" She shakes her head slowly, eyes still on the priest. "No, sister, no. We did not."

The Second Battlefront

OF COURSE, THE GOOD FIGHT was far from over. But the hit list had changed. It turned out the enemy wasn't just Satan and wickedness in high places. Modernism had come to town. And his name was Billy Graham. It was 1956, and the main subject in chapel was this popular evangelist and his slide into compromise. He had invited all religious leaders, including a Catholic bishop, to sit on his board, sit on the platform during evangelistic services. One of Dr. Bob's sayings was, "It's never right to do wrong in order to get a chance to do right." First you compromise the method, then the message. So now we needed to preach the gospel to a lost world and also take a stand against any of our brethren who had gone astray, a two-fronted battlefield.

We were told repeatedly that they weren't against Billy Graham because he left Bob Jones University. They even gave him an honorary degree years after he transferred to Wheaton College. But his fiery personal ambition had set him on the slippery slope of compromise. And someone had to speak out. And we were "it," the appointed, the anointed, the remnant.

It turned out if you are going to be true to the Lord, you must not only separate yourself from unbelievers but from those believers who associate with unbelievers, a sort of secondary separation. You could host a dinner for doctors and invite all the doctors, hold a teachers' workshop and welcome all teachers. But if you were considering marriage, founding a church or Christian school or organizing an evangelistic campaign, you could only join together with like-minded believers. Word went out to BJ pastors to stop using Billy Graham films and supporting his crusades when they came to town. Secondary separation cut another huge swath of Christendom off from fellowship and cooperation and took a lot of explaining to justify. So almost every day in chapel we got another hand-out, an open letter from Dr. Bob or the administration to another publication, pastor, denominational leader, spelling out the reason for our "stand," replete with King James Bible Scripture references. We started to bring briefcases to chapel. One wag joked that the school cooks even changed their recipes to avoid the use of graham crackers.

Pressure escalated in the waning weeks of the school year. It was imperative that we all get it, be well-versed, ready to meet the questions, the focus of the world outside when we leave for the summer, as though crowds of anxious reporters, including the religion editor of the *New York Times*, would be jostling each other at the gates, pencils poised, ready to pummel us with questions about this vital topic. But it was just our parents, trunks cleared for our dirty laundry, wondering if we had a summer job lined up.

Chapel Speaker

SOMEWHERE IN THE MIDDLE of all this frenzy came a visiting chapel speaker. I can't remember anything about him, where he was from, why he was invited to preach. But I remember his talk. He said he puzzled over what to preach about, what he could say to an audience like us, all of whom were committed Christians, many of whom already knew more about the Bible and theology than he. He felt humbled and a little intimidated even to be speaking to us. What could he say that would be meaningful?

He told us that throughout the years of his pastorate, he'd learned that whenever he was stymied as to what to say, what to do, just to say the word, "Jesus." Just speak his name. And so that's what he decided to do here today. He decided to point us to Jesus through music. Apologizing for his voice, which was thin and reedy, he stepped aside from the pulpit and started to sing all the hymns he knew that used the word "Jesus."

> Jesus, Oh, How Sweet the Name
> Jesus, Jesus, Jesus, Sweetest Name I Know
> Jesus Loves Me
> I Love to Tell the Story of Jesus and His Love

I don't know how others received this little un-sermon, this old country pastor standing there alone, hands at his sides, without accompaniment, singing to us, singing gospel songs, songs we'd heard all our lives, knew by heart, but heard freshly that day, sung by a man with a not-so-good voice who couldn't think of anything else to say, any regular three-point sermon topic. I don't know about the others, but I started a new practice. I started keeping a piece of paper in the back of the New Testament in my purse. This paper has changed over the years from a Smith Corona manually typed, to IBM Selectric, to MacIntosh word-processed, replaced when it gets faded, torn at the fold marks. But the words have stayed the same, the words of some hymns and choruses that center around the name of Jesus. When I'm stuck for myself or another, in the middle of the night alone, when life seems a bad cosmic joke, or at the hospital bed of a dying friend, I realize I don't know much theology, don't really know the Bible very well, can't pray, have nothing to say because I don't know what I know, I get out this paper. My voice is not great either, not a solo voice, but I remember that old pastor, and I sing these songs. I sing about Jesus.

Last spring a good friend of mine died, a professional actress and a devout believer. She was an avid Braves fan and chose the hospice, Our Lady of Perpetual Help, because it was so near the stadium you could hear the crowd. When Suzanne was beyond words, I sang gospel songs to her. Her daughter came into the room once and heard me singing to her and decided to do the same when it was her turn. Sue confessed at her mother's funeral that the last song she sang to her mother, the night before she died, was

> "There's no business like show business,
> Like no business I know..."

Next day on her dressing room, they hung a star.

Section V · Sixties, Early Seventies
Marrying Young

I LET MOST DECISIONS be made for me, did whatever caused the least trouble, cost the least money. You don't rock the boat when it's already sinking. So at seventeen, I was fine by the church—never drank, smoked or even dated much, unblemished and, the highest female virtue of them all, "quiet." My choice had been a fundamentalist college or no college at all, and once there I wouldn't even meet, let alone marry, anyone but a true Christian. I'd worked since I was twelve and saved nearly every cent. It was my only hope for college back before government student loans and I had a specific goal in mind: $812, one year's room, board and tuition. I'd get no financial help from home, there being two sons to educate. It was different for my friends, but this was pretty much what I'd expected.

I loved college and wanted to stay and graduate. But I'd fallen in love, and Les wanted us to marry right away. My $812 was gone, and going back home was unthinkable, like putting toothpaste back in the tube. I saved enough over the summer after my freshman year for one more quarter, but then the jig was up and a wedding date was set. Les was bright and attractive, well-liked on campus, the son of faculty members. I could picture our life together in the ministry, having children and a beautiful home like his parents had.

It was to be a modest wedding in a church I'd never even attended. When I was a child, my folks went with a group that broke off from First Baptist and started a new church. While I was away at college, they broke off from the break-off and went back to First Baptist. A week before the wedding, I was informed that I'd have to go forward at next Sunday's altar call to join the church before the wedding. What? I can't just sign something? I'm not even going to live here! No, church policy was clear; I had to go forward, meet with the deacons, give testimony and join the church.

· · · · · ·

• • •

That Sunday the preacher tells how the Lord has blessed his ministry here. Every single Sunday since he's been the pastor, nearly twelve years, someone has come forward. But this election's rigged. They sing "Just As I Am," and he gives the altar call. Come, all you sinners, all you winos and backsliders, all you brides-to-be-whose-invitations-have-already-gone-out. Come to the mourner's bench and be redeemed, get saved, get on the church rolls. We'll sing another verse.

I reluctantly go forward, shake hands with the pastor. I am led to the deacons' meeting and sit stunned. They say welcome home, as if I'd strayed, like a lost sheep, although I'd been going to a church just down the street with beliefs identical to this one. Still it wasn't home, was it? They notice my reticence and start to assure each other. "Well, of course she's born-again! I remember her with pigtails!" "Besides, she's been to Bible college, going into the ministry." Just a formality, heh, heh. The meeting adjourns quickly (the roast is in the oven), and I'm officially in.

• • •

On our wedding night, Les brings me into the motel bathroom to say that this is how he likes a bathroom to look, shiny and spotless. I'm sinking quickly. I know how to scrub a sink, but where do you get those paper strips for the toilet seats? Back home one night I wake him up in the middle of the night to say I can't breathe, I'm so afraid of dying. I can't picture married life after all, only the dead-end of my parents' relationship. We're just two penniless young people without a college degree between us. I want to be held, listened to, reassured. But he puts on his pastor's face and reaches for the big Bible on the nightstand.

Bargains

TEN MONTHS LATER, I was back in Greenville, South Carolina, again at Bob Jones University, but this time I was nineteen and pregnant. Les went to school days and worked at a gas station nights and weekends. We were poor, but so were all our friends. Our pregnant Scrabble group laughed about one of the Preacher Boy's wives whose underpants, the elastic shot, fell down around her ankles as she walked downtown. She just coolly stepped out of them and kept walking. We all had safety pins in our underwear.

Each Saturday my mother-in-law, a housewife who worked part-time at the University library, picked me up and we'd drive to Pick 'N Pay discount food market, a dark wet warehouse on the edge of town where you brought your own bags. She would dress up in a leopard stole, hat, gloves and three inch heels. I'd wear one of my three cotton maternity tops. I'd buy produce and one pound of hamburger, at 39 cents a pound, to be divided into our three meat meals for the week. When there was overtime pay I could splurge on an occasional chicken or ham hock.

Vi wanted to get groceries cheap too, but was terrified of being seen at Pick 'N Pay. From a dirt-poor family in southeast Illinois, she was obsessed with appearing richer than she was. Her clear and driving goal in life was to have the envy and respect of their acquaintances—Bob Jones colleagues, neighbors and a small independent Baptist church. She was a wizard at dressing, decorating and entertaining to look lavish even on a modest income.

So we'd shop each Saturday, quickly and furtively, she standing off to the side, never touching the cart, although a corner was reserved for her purchases. She was alert and ready to explain to anyone we might bump into that she was only here to help me out. You know how it is when you're still in college, ha, ha.

. . . . . .

The next year we were at Nyack Missionary College in New York, one of fifteen sudden moves in eighteen years, always away from something: some conflict, some mess. And I was pregnant with Pete. Our first-born, Steve, was so cute, a chubby, happy little kid who walked—ran, really—at eight months. This was more fun than I'd ever had. One afternoon, the three of us were shopping at K Mart. I could feel Les' uneasiness, very much his mother's son, bristly and prickly about being in a tacky discount store. I was heavy with child but started playing a sort of hide-and-seek with Steve in and out of the aisle. Peek! Around the corner. Boo! I don't know how I lost my balance, but suddenly I was on my back with the wind knocked out of me. I looked up to see Les, disgusted and humiliated, turn on his heel and walk in the opposite direction, pretending not to notice.

Solicitous strangers, in contrast, rushed toward me and helped me up. Their concern and kindness was water on a desert; it had been so long since anyone had treated me nicely. But I felt ashamed and had a vivid picture of how ungainly I must have looked to my husband. It was reflected so clearly in his face.

I wish now, over forty years later, one of those strangers had been an old woman, an angel sent straight from the Lord, to whisper the truth to that young girl sprawled on the K Mart floor.

Dear one, you are not drunk. You are not dirty or disgusting, just pregnant (with his child) and a little clumsy. You're young and enjoying your darling toddler—isn't he the cutest thing? You're shopping for bargains, working part time, helping your husband through school. Aren't you smart and thrifty?

What's the matter then? What's wrong with this picture?

Not you. Not you.

The Pastor's Wife's Secret

AFTER SEVEN COLLEGE TRANSFERS, Les finally got a BCE, a Bachelor's of Christian Education. He pastored a small rural Baptist church in New York state, forty miles north of New York City, and I had two boys under three. The white clapboard church was tucked into a woods in the green, lush hills described by Washington Irving in *The Legend of Sleepy Hollow.*

My eyes stung from the smoke of the wood-burning stove in the middle of the pews. The old folks sat close to it, still in hats and coats and boots. But it wasn't cold. In fact, I removed the shoes of my two toddlers. Their stocking feet made less noise that way as they played on the wooden pews, ate Cheerios and scribbled on the bulletins. I was pregnant again and needed to go to the bathroom, but I decided wait. It was an outhouse, and the seats were cold. The felt on the piano hammers had long since worn away, so the notes of the hymns in this nearly empty, sweet old church sounded tinny, like the music in a honky-tonk bar from the Old West.

Just a handful of people still gathered to worship in the Church-in-the-Woods. Over 200 years ago, when it was in its heyday, several of the 400 members were Indians. Now there were Baptist churches everywhere in this area, most born of splits. They're like children and grandchildren, descendants of this church. And they never write. How did this place survive with so few members led by student pastors? I thought maybe those who died, who founded it and nurtured it through the years, still held it up with their prayers and good wishes.

For some reason I became obsessed with the idea that I wanted to do something "for the Lord," something that was anonymous, had no connection with the church. I already did a lot, and it was all pleasant: teach Sunday school, bake pies for the deacons' meetings, type the bulletin and run it off the moist and drippy mimeograph machine. And I'd even learned to play the organ. When someone wanted to donate an organ to the church, another person asked, "Who will play it?" The answer was, "Well, it comes with three free lessons!" So I became the church organist, hoping against hope that nobody would invite a real musician to church. But everything I did was connected to my husband's work. So I started praying for the chance to do something apart from my role as a minister's wife.

I was invited to a shower, and the guests included some folks from the community who didn't go to our church.

I learned that Mary's elderly mother, a diabetic who had gone blind and was confined to a wheelchair, spent her days alone while Mary and her husband worked. She was very lonely and discouraged.

I resolved to call her, but to keep my identity vague. If I thought I'd taken on an onerous chore to experience holy suffering, I was quickly disabused. We hit it off from the start. She served in World War I as a nurse and had wonderful stories. She'd been a big reader, and we had many favorite authors in common. I read passages to her out of my current library book from the county bookmobile (thank you, Andrew Carnegie). I called her each weekday afternoon, during the kids' nap-time, and we got on famously, laughing and chatting like old buddies. I told no one, not even my husband.

One day she said she really missed music. "This house has no music in it." The next day, I tuned up my violin, propped the phone receiver on the piano and played anything she wanted in the hymnbook, up to two sharps. Each phone call ended with a hymn or two. We kept each other merry company through a cold and snowbound winter. Even when a group of us went to her house Christmas caroling, I kept my distance and didn't introduce myself.

One Sunday, I heard two women at church talking. "How's Mary's mother doing?"

"Not well. Not well at all. They may have to put her back in the home."

My heart sank, and I moved closer to eavesdrop. "What's wrong?" "Well, now her mind is really going. She says someone—she doesn't know who—calls her every day and plays the violin."

Evangelizing Maria

GEORGE BOUTELIER WAS A REAL TROPHY for Second Baptist, a nearby church, and its pastor, the Rev. Wayne Harrison and his wife, Esther. For he was that rarest phenomenon, a true adult convert. George, an alcoholic and lapsed Catholic, managed a shoe store in Carmel, had a wife, two kids and one on the way. He was a likable fellow. We were all taken by him. His wife, Maria, was wonderful too, happy and friendly, but quieter than George and a little shy. They were crazy about each other. He wanted her to be saved too, especially before the baby was born. So we all prayed she would be.

Maria came to church Sunday mornings, but that was all. Said evening service was too much for her, pregnant and with small children. George pointed out that other women do it. "But I'm not used to this." He started to pressure her. "You need to come Sunday nights." Maria just smiled and promised maybe next week.

George and the pastor and other church people started to zero in on Maria. Wouldn't she like to receive Christ as her Savior? "I'm already a Christian—I'm a Catholic." But it's not the same! You need to be born again, receive Christ as your Savior. "I already know he's my Savior." Have you been born again? "I'm a Catholic, we believe a little differently from that, say it differently. But it's the same thing, loving the Lord and serving him." But the Catholic Church is so corrupt, they point out, and she doesn't go there anyway. "That's true. I'm coming to church with George now. It's easier. We only have one car, and this means a lot to him."

Maria was very gracious. "I'm glad he's found the Lord. He's so happy, and it's helped him stop drinking. He just loves going to church all the time and studying his Bible. It's certainly changed him." Wouldn't you like to be changed too? "Not really. I'd like to be a better person, but I'm working on that." They quote Scripture, "Not by might nor by power, but by my Spirit, saith the Lord...." and the weeks went by.

. . . . . .

The pastor's invitations became more specific. "You need to come Sunday night and get under conviction."

"For what?"

"For your sins."

"Hey, I'm a Catholic—I know about my sins!" (Laughter all around). The months went by. She stood firm. "I'm a different type of person. I'm a Christian, too, but believe a little differently." When the church people kindly pointed out that doctrinally the Catholic Church is way off, Maria asked outright, "You can't be a Christian unless you're a Baptist? Everyone in the whole world is going to hell but Baptists?"

Well, of course, they didn't mean that. "But you haven't received Christ as your personal Savior."

Maria replied, "You keep saying those words like a key, a formula, receive Christ as your personal Savior. Are those words even in the Bible?"

The time of her delivery drew nigh. She was a high risk pregnancy. The church leaders wanted to know if something happened during childbirth, would she go to heaven?

"I think so."

Wouldn't she like to know so? Doesn't she want to be 100 percent certain?

"Well, to tell you the truth, I've always thought that only crazy people are 100 percent certain of anything. Childbirth is hard and scary, and I don't want to worry about going to hell too! You know, I can't just make myself believe something. You believe what you believe. I believe once a Catholic, always a Catholic."

But do you know Christ as your personal Savior?

"Maybe," she replies. "Could you hum a few bars?"

We moved (of course) while Maria was still holding out. I heard that she joined the church some time after the baby was born. I don't know whether she had a change of heart or just wanted some peace and quiet.

. . . . . .

Elrod, New York

I LIKED ELROD. It was a beautiful little town in western New York State with lots of old trees, sidewalks, a white bandstand, red brick churches and a genuine, all-purpose five-and-dime store. I didn't particularly like Elrod Baptist, which was a problem because my husband was the pastor. I was glad to be out of the isolation of the country, but didn't want to live above a storefront church with three little kids and a big dog. The only place to play and hang clothes outdoors was a flat rooftop without a railing. The man who founded the church, the Rev. Don Draper, did so because of a disagreement with First Baptist, where all his relatives, including his wife and children, still went. The Rev. Draper was an ordained minister who wanted someone to pastor his little flock because he was going on to bigger and better things, selling life insurance. He insisted he was still in the ministry, was adamant about being addressed as "Reverend" and still felt entitled to clergy discounts from local merchants. He wasn't in business in the strictest sense of the word, after all, because the insurance company was Baptist Life Assemblage. He put together two verses: "Forsake not the assembling of yourselves together," which meant really good Christians even buy their insurance together, and, "A workman is worthy of his hire," justifying the huge commissions which helped him build a big new house with a pool just outside town.

So we moved and settled in. (Well, I waited in Nyack four months until school was out so Steve wouldn't have to go to three first grades). The first Sunday of the month they received new members and, evidently, this month, that was us. If I had thought the pastor and his wife, living upstairs on a shoestring to serve this tiny parish, were automatically received as members, I was mistaken. There were rules. Procedures. These people, all fifteen of them, had standards.

. . . . . .

The two deacons and the Rev. Draper and Les and I met after the evening service. Les gave his testimony, a clear-cut conversion experience, which easily passed muster. His parents were born again when he was entering adolescence, and they all moved to Bob Jones University, a dramatic change from the nightclub scene where his dad played sax in a dance band. It more than passed muster—it got an A+. Then the Rev. Draper's sights were turned on me. Well, hmm. My dad was a Baptist minister, so I was always in church, sort of always believed. I was baptized by immersion at four. He wondered aloud if a four-year-old really knew enough, could understand enough, to be sure of her salvation at such a tender age. I couldn't really recall exactly what I knew at that age.

Could I name another date, later, a time of decision making, of giving my heart to the Lord? Not really. I remembered a lot of emotional altar calls, youth rallies and sentimental end-of-camp campfires, but nothing specific. I just knew I was Christian, a believer. I read my Bible and believed it but had no date written in the fly-leaf. Well, that was all well and good, but not quite good enough. And the more he probed, the more vague I became.

We were at an impasse. He was not satisfied, and I wasn't budging from my story, or lack of it. A little voice inside said that he could hardly keep the pastor's wife out and, of course, I didn't really want to be in anyway. We'd already been called on by the Presbyterian pastor and his wife, a congenial couple I took to immediately. Their church was just down the block....

After a long, awkward silence in which we just stared at each other, he asked in exasperation, "Well, is there a day you can point to when you knew for sure you were a Christian?"

"Yes, today."

Meeting adjourned.

Section VI • Late Seventies
Parking Lots I Have Known

NEXT TIME I HAVE A NERVOUS BREAKDOWN, I'm choosing a nicer place. I had mine in downtown Atlanta, ninety-five degrees, in the parking decks at Georgia State University. With all the moves, it had taken me ten years to get an undergraduate degree, and I was in graduate school part-time. As I searched each floor of the decks for my car (three stories in one structure, four in another, and I didn't even know which building I'd parked in), I sat down on the metal stairs between floors and cried. It was so long overdue that once I started, I couldn't stop. I thought, if someone finds me like this, they'll take me across the street to the Grady Hospital psych ward.

It had been a long four years since I'd learned, on our fourteenth wedding anniversary, that Les was in love with a teen in our church youth group. Our marriage had always been rocky, but the infidelity surprised me. When Claire's parents found out, we had to move fast and far. Maybe a move to Atlanta would be a fresh start. But it was happening again, and this time I broke—working full time, going to graduate school nights, and, most exhausting of all, trying to pretend everything was okay.

When I finally found my car, I went straight to an old friend. She came to the door all dressed up with her pearls on, ready to go out, but when she saw my face, she said, "You're the only important thing right now." And the whole grade-B movie poured out, the shame, the shame.

The next morning, while he was shaving, I sat on the edge of the tub and told Les what I had done, about breaking down and going to my friend. I knew he'd be mad, but I wasn't ready for the outburst of shock and anger. Now I'd blown it: it was all over now; now I'd done it. I guess when all a couple has left is facade, whoever lets one person, even a discreet friend, behind the scenes spoils the illusion and creates an irreparable breach.

That same hot summer of 1977, the mayor of Atlanta, in his infinite wisdom, decided to meet the energy crisis head on with a *two*-hour time change called Extra Daylight Savings Time. My own life was already so far out of whack that this additional adjustment really threw me, made my life surreal, having to cross a time zone to get to Kroger.

Les was working as a claims adjuster. I was managing a counseling center on Lenox Road, across from Lenox Square. I couldn't afford a parking spot under the office building. My only alternative was to park at Les' work about four blocks away and walk. I started work at six in the morning so I could be home by two mainly, it seemed, in order to take someone to the emergency room. My kids, ten, twelve and fourteen, were having a contest that summer to see who could get the most stitches.

It wasn't merely dark when I went to work that early; it felt like the middle of the night. I kept checking my watch. It could have been midnight instead of 5:30 A.M. And, since Les' current infatuation worked at his office, too, I was scared of seeing something in the company parking lot I shouldn't. So I'd drive to work in pitch dark, park and, eyes straight ahead, walk up Lenox Road. One morning I felt as low as I'd ever been, utterly alone and hopeless. You can live with pain, but not without hope. The world had suddenly become eerie and sinister, every tree a shadow, every shadow a hiding place. I was petrified.

Two old black women came out of an office building with their buckets and cleaning supplies and ambled up Lenox Road in front of me toward the bus stop. One said something that tickled the other, and she started in giggling a low giggle. The other laughed at her in response and their hilarity bounced off each other and escalated from a hee-hee-hee to a full-blown belly laugh. Just as it would die down, a small chuckle would surface, and they'd lose it again. When they noticed me behind them and realized how dopey they must

· · · · · ·

look, it set them off on new rounds of side-splitting laughter. By now they were holding on to each other, lamp posts, mailboxes, anything to keep from falling down on the sidewalk. Our progress up Lenox Road had nearly slowed to a halt.

I shook my head to show my "disapproval" of their scandalous behavior and that struck them as even funnier. Their laughter was as contagious as a yawn, and by the time I reached my office building, I was laughing as hard as they were, which tickled them even more, because this stupid white woman didn't even hear the original joke.

In an instant, everything had changed. I rode up in the elevator alone, feeling renewed, refreshed, relaxed and in love, not with a person, but with this morning, this world and those two old ladies holding on to the lamp post. I loved my life and could hardly wait to live it.

Nothing changed at home, of course. That fall, Les started looking at apartments, but said he wouldn't move out until after the Christmas holidays; it was little like having an appendectomy a scratch at a time. Then, when he moved out, the only thing he did for us was make the mortgage payments on the house, which was in his name. The bills quickly piled up beyond my small income. I had to hire a lawyer and sue for child support, using the word "separation," until he helped me begin to use the "d" word. This time, when Les started the "now you've done it" routine, I thought to myself, but didn't say, never did say, "No, you killed it. I'm just making funeral arrangements."

· · · · · ·

The Phone Book Trick

WHEN DOES A MARRIAGE END? Usually not with a bang, but with a whimper. With me, it was a small piece of paper, a receipt. We'd been close to bankruptcy before, and this time, since the boys were older and I was working full-time, the lenders insisted on my signature. I didn't want to co-sign another loan, borrowing just to keep afloat. I wanted to cut back and slowly pay off the bills we had. But the specter of bankruptcy scared me, so, after he promised we'd tear up the credit cards and live on our income until this loan was paid off, I signed the papers. A couple of weeks later, I picked up a shopping bag to throw away and a small white credit card receipt fell out. By the time it touched the ground, I was divorced. The price of a pair of khakis isn't much compared to the other broken promises, but that's when I lost hope, all trust in a future together.

When a marriage ends and the circumstances come to light, the first question outsiders usually wonder about is, why didn't she just leave? Well, first of all, even in an unhappy marriage, there are good times of affection and reconciliation that give hope for change. And, more importantly, a believer always takes seriously a promise to God. So how did things for these two Christians get so far out of whack?

I read once that the secret to tearing a phone book in half is the angle. If you can hold the book at just the right angle, you're really just tearing it one page at a time. When I tried to think back and understand how Les got such a hold on me, on all of us, so that we were always on the defensive, on edge, I thought maybe it was the angle. When we met, he was three years older, an experienced junior, whose folks were on the university staff, well known and liked. They lived near campus in a lovely house, wore stylish clothes, had the charming aura of winners. I was a sixteen-year-old freshman from an unstable home, with a drop-out dad and a house that was nearly falling apart in body and spirit. My parents and

· · · · · ·

my life were clearly inferior to his glamorous parents and their star status on campus. Add to that inequality all the church's teaching about women being in submission to their husbands, and the balance of power is skewed from the get-go.

And the angle held, one thin, tearable edge at a time—I trying to please, make the grade, but always falling short. The scrutiny was on me: my looks, my housekeeping skills, my lack of social graces. If the criticism keeps coming, all one-way, nobody ever thinks to turn the tables and say, "What about you?"

The first infidelity was so jarring, I think that's when the tearing lost its angle. Then, four years later, a few weeks after he had left for good, he called to say we needed to talk, that maybe we could have a "date." I felt so awkward. Do I dress up? I never pleased him before. In fact, when he left, he said the main thing was my looks, that I'd never developed the way he thought I would. He wanted someone "stunning." Stunning.

So now we had a "date." I got into his new car, and by the time we drove one block to the corner, he said, "You really need to cream your neck, the skin is dry and old-looking." I still had my hand on the car door handle. We were stopped at a stop sign, and it occurred to me that I could just open the door and get out, walk home. But I didn't. Why not? Lack of nerve? Habit? Didn't want, even then, to make a scene? Or did I stay out of curiosity? He said he wanted to talk; what did he want to say? In any case, I stayed but couldn't help thinking his dating skills could use some brushing up.

He asked me where we could go for a drink. We've never been people who "go out for a drink," so I had no idea. He had been going out with the guys after work and to singles places for a long time. But his world had changed, and mine had not. We drove to a nearby place, Alexander Eagle, but when we opened the bar door, the music was too loud. He whirled around, and I followed him back to the car. It has always been this. He acts, reacts, changes his mind, and I follow in his wake, wondering what's next. I was suddenly aware of how helpless I felt, like plankton.

. . . . . .

We drove to a place he knew, a motel lounge, and it was quiet. We got a table, sat down and ordered drinks. I remembered a friend of mine who, trying to be sophisticated in a bar for the first time, ordered a "whiskey and bourbon." So I played it safe and just asked for white wine. How am I doing? Fine. How is he doing? Fine. I took a deep breath and realized I felt okay. It was an awkward situation for both of us and yet, surprisingly, I felt fine, somewhat removed, my arms resting on the chair arms, not leaning on the table. Nothing connects us. I'm over here. He's over there, asking what do I think.

What do I think? I think there are many ways to be a good husband and father and many roles to play: provider, protector, lover, spiritual head of the family, handyman, lifter of heavy objects. And when I look back on our life together, I don't remember getting very much of that support or husbanding. But I didn't speak in anger. I said what I had to say about the experience of being married to him, what it felt like to look around and see other wives, many who weren't trying nearly as hard as I, treated like assets while I felt like a liability. To see our friends' children treasured and ours, every bit as bright and dear, dragged around like so much baggage. To never put my whole weight down for fear the base would give. To lie awake at night planning my newest fire escape plan for yet another house, then waking up each morning to wonder which state we're in. To watch other men sometimes turn down a promotion because uprooting the kids would be too traumatic. To work at a Christian counseling center and watch a parade of doctors, lawyers and even prominent pastors— husbands—humble themselves and come in for marriage counseling. But not mine. No, I guessed, we can't work things out.

Turkey in April

FOUR MONTHS LATER, Steve returned from working with a puppet ministry in the Bronx during his spring break from college. For his first dinner home, I made his favorites, turkey and dressing with all the trimmings. As soon as he got back from visiting his dad, we sat down to eat. We held hands and, during the blessing, I expressed thanks that our family was back together again. As soon as the prayer ended, Steve said, "But we're not all together. Dad isn't here. He says he wants to come back, but you won't let him." I was stunned. I looked at the other two boys. Their eyes were fastened on me and I realized that their dad had been talking to them privately about coming home.

Something in me snapped. I was so mad that I reached right over for the phone and called Les, told him to come over immediately. He asked what it was about, said he had "commitments." But I was adamant.

The meal forgotten, we went into the living room and Les soon arrived. I told him that the boys had the impression he was going to come back home, that we possibly were going to get back together. He said, well, he'd been meaning to talk to me about that. He thought maybe we could work something out. I wanted him to tell the boys why that wasn't possible, why the marriage was over. I offered to leave as he talked to them but said I thought they deserved the truth. He said not to leave, but told them in the vaguest possible terms that he had done some things which caused me not to be able to trust him any more. And he was the one who had caused the break-up, had changed, and not to blame me. Then he left.

The boys all went upstairs and, after a short while, Steve came back down. "I still don't get it." It was the seventies, and a book called *Open Marriage* was on the bestseller list. I told Steve about the premise of the book, that some people believed a marriage commitment

. . . . . .

needn't be monogamous, two people loving only each other. And some people could live in an open marriage, but I couldn't. I began to cry. I didn't want to say any of this, didn't want to say anything against their dad. But I felt backed into a corner and so explained it on a theoretical level, the old term paper approach. Steve said, "Okay, now I get it. But you should have said something sooner." He went upstairs and talked to Pete and Chris. I never knew what he said to them. But when they all came to the dining room, we sat down and ate huge helpings of cold turkey and stuffing. It was delicious, and from then on I was queen.

From the Pew

LATE FIFTIES:

Our little church is independent, too pure to even associate with any Baptist convention, not accountable to any organization or hierarchy. "Accountable only to the Lord," is our motto, with the Bible as our "only rule for faith and practice."

My husband is a good preacher, passionate and eloquent, and the church is growing, buying a bus, hosting a local radio program and even putting in an indoor toilet. But my life is full of pain. He hates it here and strikes out at us, his family. Today I wear long sleeves to cover a bruise. A woman comes up to me after church and says, "We just love your husband. I thank the Lord for him every day."

LATE SIXTIES:

The Jesus Movement is upon us, and instead of a small Sunday school class of recalcitrant teens whose parents made them come, we've had to move the class to the "Y" to accommodate the crowds. Les, as Youth Pastor, forms a chorale of young people to go on tour for the summer, through all the New England states, singing at sedate, rural Lutheran churches, which the three busloads of teenagers hit like a firestorm. *Jesus Christ, Super Star*. All of a sudden being in church work is cool, and everything we do is right, blessed. Open a coffee house, and it's SRO every night.

But there are midnight calls from parents and a constant stream of teens in trouble: suicide attempts, sex, drug abuse, runaways, so Les has time for everyone but family, and I have to go to another school concert and watch a son's face fall when he spots the empty seat next to me. Reporters are coming to the "Y" this Wednesday night, and Les will not miss that for anything.

. . . . . .

On Sundays, I listen to the young people give testimonies in church. The star is Claire, a sixteen-year-old convert from Catholicism. People are saved every Sunday. The older folks, while a little startled by all the hoopla, are pleased. Once again, I field compliments. What a wonderful man your husband is. He's made such a difference in our son.

We have our picture taken for the staff section of the new church directory. The photographer says, "What a beautiful family!"

Three days after Christmas, on our fourteenth wedding anniversary, he and Claire tell me they are in love. "We didn't mean for this to happen. We both care about you." Already they're a "we." For my birthday in January, he gives me a suitcase.

Claire isn't a beauty, but she has a waif-like charm and a coat with buttons missing. After nearly a year, she confides in her sister, trying to borrow money to run away. Her sister tells their parents, and Les and I are summoned to a meeting. They are sending her to a private high school in Buffalo, but Les says that's not far enough; they'd still get together. So we start to pack for Atlanta.

LATE SEVENTIES:

I'm going to give this one last try. It could go either way. A priest at an Episcopal church near the counseling center where I work calls often and refers someone in crisis. "Don't worry about the bill." But then it turns out they don't worry about it either, and I have to call the church office about the past-due accounts. The priest has a nice voice, and I grow curious about this little church with a heart bigger than its pocketbook. I start to go but sit in the back, arrive late and leave early because the sermons are good and the ritual and music are sufficiently unfamiliar. If I take some Benadryl beforehand and leave before the Doxology, maybe I won't get hives. If this doesn't work out, I'll give up. I've got a wonderful husband now, and he's not a churchgoer. I have plenty of Christian friends. The kids are

. . . . . .

away at college. And if I stay home Sunday mornings, reading the paper on the deck with my new husband, the Lord will understand. It will be okay.

But I feel drawn to this church, this priest. Before he preaches, the custom is to pray for him and bless him with outstretched hands. I want to fit in, so I do the same from my back pew. But I'm really praying for myself, a secret personal ritual. I will my left hand, with its direct connection to my heart, to open and receive. To be here and now, not there and then. To hear the Word and not the echo. Then I tap my chest bone twice, skin on skin. This is me. I'm here. I'm alive, in this pew. What'cha got for me?

It will be a couple of years before I get around to praying for the priest.

Easter, 1979

SPRING OF 1979 was a sweet and easy time for me: a new husband, a new deck and they started home delivery of the *New York Times* in Atlanta. My kids were pretty much grown. After years of bruising church experiences, I felt overdue for a lengthy sabbatical. I read my Bible and prayed each morning. I was still a believer. I just wanted a break from church. I imagined Sunday mornings with my husband on the deck that overlooked our woodsy little valley, watching the bunny eat my basil while I leafed through the thick book section of the *Times.* Oh, joy.

But it was Easter, and I decided to check out a small Episcopal church in our neighborhood. It met in a rectangular, cinder block building with clangy folding chairs, not much different from the Church of the Open Door. They also had tippy wooden kneeling benches, but I didn't intend to use them anyway. The sermon that first Sunday at St. Patrick's Episcopal Church was on all the people named in the Bible during Christ's Passion—that's it, just named. Never mentioned before or after, did nothing worth recording, just onlookers.

I'd been listening to Dr. Martin Luther King's sermons on tape in my car and thought of his words about justice issues coming to crises. "I just want to be there. I want it said of me, 'he was there.'"

The priest said that if you are present where things are happening, where the Spirit is moving and working, maybe some of it will rub off on you. Maybe you'll get in on the action, and maybe you won't. But just being there, bearing witness, is enough, is plenty, is essential. If you're not there, you'll miss out.

Rub off on you. It sounded just passive enough for me. I was tired of the good fight, weary of keeping steady. When it came to church, I was an empty well with nothing to give, my faith more questions than answers, an authority on nothing. But I thought I could do that. I thought I wanted to do that, be there in the last pew. Show up. Just to see what happened.

Section VII • Eighties

Heaven's Gain

ONE MORNING, a few years after I'd joined St. Patrick's, my husband, Bill, called from his office down the street to say he was bringing me a surprise. He'd met an old friend of mine. We had known each other at Bob Jones University in the fifties. Bill left, and Jan and I talked and laughed and cried together like old war vets and suddenly Bill reappeared. My usually gracious husband blurted out, "Are you still here?" And we laughed again to see it was after five.

Jan was from southeast Alabama and was sent off to Bob Jones Academy to get "straightened out." It didn't work, and she had fallen for pretty Carol Bryant, also a high school junior. Someone saw something, and Jan was sent to the Dean of Education, a piece of luck, because he was a rare bird on that campus—quiet, compassionate and merciful. He gave her some statistics from Kinsey to show that many adolescents, especially from loveless homes, have homosexual "crushes," that she wasn't a freak. And she would almost surely grow out of it. "But don't do that any more."

Jan threw herself into studies and extra curricular activities and, in her senior year, was voted "Spirit of Bob Jones Academy," the top honor. She entered BJU, and once more someone saw something, and she was "shipped." Her mom had her committed against her will to the Alabama state insane asylum in Huntsville for two years. "I fell in love, so they locked me up. My mom knew the judge."

After she got out, she moved to Georgia and took up church work again. She was made for Christian Ed. Someone once gave her a T-shirt, "Born to Skit." Jan had it all: energy, joy

. . . . . .

and an abundant love of people and the Lord. She was big, loud, boisterous and laughed at the beginning of your joke. And she adored Roy Rogers.

Once she co-directed a Daily Vacation Bible School in the inner city of Atlanta with another BJU alum, a fellow she liked quite a lot. One night he stayed over. They watched her favorite Roy Rogers movie on television, and then they tried making love. But he was gay too, and they ended up laughing so hard he fell out of bed. They went to sleep snuggling and the next morning joked that now they had to get married since they'd slept together. Later they did discuss the possibility—a dual cover-up so they could stay in Christian ministry to which they both felt called. But the discussion didn't last long, because they giggled too much.

Then Jan met Mary. The two lived happily together for seven years. Mary was "the best thing that ever happened to me," Jan said. I never knew why they broke up. Jan finally gave up on the evangelical church. "I've been celibate for five years, and they still don't want me." She went into insurance where she met my husband.

Jan and I had great times together after we met again. We'd both been through the cold, narrow blades of fundamentalism and come out the other side still believers: I in the Episcopal Church and Jan in a little house church she deeply loved.

Once she asked a favor of me. Next time Bill and I went out in public for the day, shopping, or to a fair or festival, would I try not touching him? Try pretending to be just platonic friends, no hand-holding or demonstrations of affection. I tried and failed and saw how hard it would be to be in love with someone and keep your distance, keep it all under wraps.

A few years ago, Jan stayed with us during an Overeaters' Anonymous convention at a hotel near our house. She had a hot pink Little Bo-Peep costume left over from Halloween, and we wrote a skit, like in the old days. It started with her yawning, awakening from a nap, looking around for her sheep. "Where are those suckers?" Then wondering aloud why she was so hungry for mint jelly. It brought the house down. She ended by singing a ditty I wrote to the tune of "The Whiffenpoof Song." One verse went,

> ... tripling every recipe,
> even Elephant Fricassee!
> Lord, have mercy on such as we,
> Baaah, baaah, baaah ...

In late spring, she left a message on my machine that she was in the hospital and very sick. I was out of the country and by the time I got back, she was almost gone. All I could do was sit by her bed and sing to her. I went through every verse of every hymn or Sunday school song I knew that centered around the name of Jesus. "Oh, How I Love Jesus!," "Jesus Loves Me," "Jesus, Jesus, Jesus, Sweetest Name I Know." I was so grateful for our early years which had left us a rich heritage of sweet old gospel songs, words to live by and die by.

> Soon He's coming back to welcome me
> Far beyond the starry sky.
> I shall wing my flight to worlds unknown,
> I shall reign with Him on high.

She died of cancer that June, one week after her fiftieth birthday. Her beloved sister, Nancy, with whom she'd lived the last fifteen years, was in charge of the funeral. Mary came from Alabama. We sang, "Amazing Grace" and "Happy Trails to You."

· · · · · ·

My Shabbat Rebbe

I'VE NEVER LIKED SUNDAYS. As early as I can remember, when I woke up and realized it was Sunday, my heart dropped and my stomach crunched. Our family did better to all go our separate ways, as we did on weekdays—until dinner. Sitting in that small, cramped kitchen (the roomy dining room table, just six feet away, was reserved for company) was torture. We said an awkward, perfunctory grace, followed by long, hard silences until we'd eaten enough to be excused—early release. But Sunday, we faced the double whammy: the family-at-home-together and church. Tense getting ready, tense at church and then tense family dinner at Grandpa Keiffer's house—lots of smoke, competition and keen ridicule.

As a young adult, Sundays meant all those shoes to polish, even more tension and angry outbursts and then, finally at church, trying to act nicer and happier than I was: scrutinizing time. Mondays were such a relief—a whole week ahead of just the kids and me left alone to enjoy each other.

But one August a few years ago, I was challenged by a sermon to rethink the concept of the Sabbath. I guess I'd taken for granted that going to church on Sunday and not working at a job constituted "keeping the Sabbath." I avoided shopping or doing chores on Sunday. That's enough, right? But, as I took another look, I realized my ideas were fuzzy and unexamined, formed more by culture and family background than spiritual discernment. And I saw, as I looked at Scripture, that not only was keeping the Sabbath not optional, it was, with the exception of providing for the poor, the most consistent and concrete imperative throughout the Old and New Testaments. Oops! The preacher suggested that the day of the week probably didn't even matter and that the agenda was to be, well, absent, just a time to "kick back and goof off." I drew a blank. Had I lost the use of those muscles? More likely I'd never developed them. Outside of playing some with my kids when they were young, I'd been pretty much a drag.

Two other things were happening in my life that August. My brother, Ken, and his wife, parents of Killian-light-of-my-life, were separating. Kim had to get a job and put Killian, three, in daycare.

At the same time, I read a book called *The Artist's Way,* which advocated writing three Morning Pages a day and taking an Artist Date weekly, a solitary time of fun and foolishness to change gears and nourish and heal the artist within. The Morning Pages were almost easy. I'd always gotten up early to journal and pray and read the Scripture. But at the Artist Date, I drew a blank. A date with myself? I can do better than that!

Kim arranged daycare for Killian on Mondays, Wednesdays and Fridays. Ken would take her to his hair dressing shop on Tuesdays, a slow day. Kim wanted to know if I would watch her on Thursdays. I jumped at the chance. I'd been wanting more time with Killian and suspected that maybe this could be the answer to my Sabbath/Artist Date quest.

Thursdays quickly became my favorite day. I'd plan all week for it. Over time, I stocked an arts and crafts cupboard, collected flea market bargains for a dress-up closet, made flags, parachutes and a puppet theater. Getting ready was half the fun.

How did we spend/waste our time together? Let me count the ways. We sat in mud puddles in the pouring rain and squirted each other with turkey basters; dropped food coloring on white platters of milk and blew it around with straws; floated leaf boats down the gutter, made Rice Krispie Treats in the shapes of dinosaurs, flopped in the hammock and made up knock knock jokes; drew each others' corpses on the sidewalk, "X" marking where the bullet went through. We made fingerpaints out of colored banana pudding, using graham crackers as brushes and eating the soggy part to get a fresh edge. We planned scary, spooky puppet shows for family get-togethers, paraded around the cul-de-sac with a boom box playing Sousa and waving six-foot flags, stood on the interstate overpass and made trucks blow their horns. We warmed clay in our underwear, dressed up in fancy clothes and hats and walked to Dairy Queen, froze a fake eyeball in an ice cube for Bill's drink, made gingerbread men and women for equal rights, invited people to a rice restaurant stocked with nothing but a washbasin of raw rice and our imagination.

Some days we'd go from project to project, finishing nothing and never, ever cleaning up after ourselves. Some days we didn't do anything but watch the clouds and make up silly songs, including an opera called, "I Hate Baloney," to the music from Carmen:

> Don't make me any baloney sandwiches
> I won't eat them because ...
> they're full of worms and bugs
> and snails and slugs
> and only thugs/eat/them.

When the student is ready, the teacher will appear.

Sick Bay

MY FAVORITE FOUR-YEAR-OLD, Killian, has come over, too sick to go to daycare, not sick enough for Mom to stay home from work. This isn't our usual day, the Thursday where we play and do art, the Sabbath I set aside just to have fun, blow bubbles and name clouds. This is a work day, and my to-do list is crammed full; several appliances are already running. This isn't Thursday. But she is four and won't understand that.

I set up the sofa ahead of time with pillows and the flower quilt we made together. I set out snacks and the TV remote, hoping to distract her from my inattention.

I sit with her awhile and we talk, but then I need to get busy. I start her drawing a butterfly and go to finish an article. When I hurry back toward the kitchen, she sits in front of a blank sheet. "Aren't you going to watch me draw?"

"I'm busy now."

"I'll wait," and she patiently puts down the crayon and looks at me expectantly. So I stop and watch a while, set out a new puzzle and some more books and take off again.

"Barbara?"

I'm getting impatient now. The area around the sofa has become an avalanche of toys, art materials and snacks, offerings I've brought to the altar of this beloved demigod. "What do you want?" She pats the space next to her and I reluctantly stop and sit and read her one story while she leans limp and heavy on my shoulder. Then the phone rings, and I absolutely have to get it. On my next trip through the living room, I see in my peripheral vision those eyes following me.

Dear one, can't you see all I've done for you, all I've bought and made and put together and cooked? The crusts I've cut off, the tuna salad I took the celery out of, the homemade applesauce? Can't you understand, your royal heiny-ness, I can't just lounge around and be with you. I need to do stuff—good stuff, important stuff, deadlines to meet, promises to keep.

Good Lord, don't you see how much I care and sacrifice and do and give? I've loved mercy, done justice, and walked humbly before you. What is it that you require of me?

Pat, pat ....

Ben

I WAS FLYING HOME from Mexico, and the friend next to me, in the window seat, was Ben Fishbein, an insurance agent and converted Jew. He was fervently explaining to me that the Old Testament pointed to Jesus, that when it spoke of the Messiah, it foretold Jesus!

In addition to his ardent evangelical belief, and enmeshed in it, was a vehement conviction that: the hopeless decline of public education was a direct result of people like Madelyn Murray O'Hare and the Supreme Court's ban on school prayers...conspiracy theories explained JFK's assassination...and nearly all current trends, pending legislation and stock market fluctuations had a direct tie-in with some verse in the Book of Revelation. He knew Hal Lindsay's books on prophecy by heart and was in great demand as a speaker at Bible studies, adult Sunday school classes and groups of "concerned" parents.

As his monologue increased in volume, scope and intensity, I became aware of a wondrous sight out the window behind his head. In all my years of air travel before or since, I've never seen anything like it—a spectacular display of clouds, brilliant in the sun, swooping and billowing in dramatic peaks and valleys. It was like seeing the Grand Canyon next to the Matterhorn. The almost-blinding light filled the cabin of the plane with an eerie glow as though we'd flown into another dimension in one of the C.S. Lewis *Chronicles of Narnia* stories. A silence settled over the other passengers as we all became mesmerized.

I tried to keep an attentive expression on my face, looking back and forth between this anxious man and this breathtaking vista that seemed to go on without end. Finally I said, "Ben, wait. Excuse me just a second. Look out there." He turned around and looked. To his credit, he went speechless.

After a few minutes, I asked the back of his head, "Do you really think the Lord who made that tells Hal Lindsay the future?"

He sighed. "Well, I don't know...but...people really eat that stuff up!"

Section VIII • Nineties–2000

I.C.U.

THE CALL CAME WHILE I was downtown getting my hair cut by my brother at his shop. Mom said to come right away, so we guess Dad is dying. I went next door to buy some spare underpants and a toothbrush while Ken phoned the airlines. We took the MARTA train to the airport at the same time that celebrating crowds crushed aboard to attend the parade honoring the Atlanta Braves, who have just won the 1992 National League Pennant. A little boy in a Braves cap stared at me while I cried into the pole I was hanging on to.

We flew to Florida, and someone met us at the airport and took us directly to the hospital, where Mom and my other brother, Jim, from Ohio, sat in the I.C.U. waiting room. Dad was out of surgery, but we hadn't heard anything yet. What kind of surgery? I didn't know. Concrete information was always hard to come by in my family. But my mother had a lot to say about these other people in the waiting room who continue to bring in food, even though the sign clearly says no food allowed. "See?" she said, pointing to the sign and then indicating yet another scofflaw balancing a box of pizza. She shook her head and clicked her tongue. We all looked at the rogues, the rule-breakers, eating chicken with their hands. Who do they think they are, flaunting authority when so much is at stake here? Not that we really believed there is any direct connection between being well-mannered and law-abiding and my dad's chances, but I have noticed that people are exceptionally polite in a hospital. And we were in the ICU waiting room, the hardest wait of all. We leafed through old magazines, played Rook, whispered to each other, "Would you like some coffee?" (Coffee is okay, a pot just outside the door.) Hours went by. And the phone stayed silent. By early evening, although no one actually admitted it, it looked as if we were going to have to go back to Mom's trailer without hearing any news.

. . . . . .

I decided to take a walk. They looked up, startled, anchored to their seats. What if someone comes, and they can't find me? The doctor could call at any minute. "I'll just go for a little walk." I found the patient unit with its sign: No Admittance, and, luckily, a nurse was coming out. I told her I was Bill Ross's daughter and would like to see him before I went home for the night. She said, "Oh, certainly," and stepped aside to let me in. I looked back to see that Ken had followed me, suspecting I was up to something. I signaled him to go get the others, and I entered the room.

All eight beds were occupied, four on either side of the nurse's station, and, although I had no idea which bed was Dad's, I ran to the farthest one on the left, some terror calling me. I wasn't even sure it was him until I saw the long feet sticking straight up. He was swathed in bandages and surrounded by tubes and equipment. His eyes flashed back and forth, back and forth. I bent close to his ear and started talking loudly and clearly. "You're going to be okay. You've had surgery, but it's over and you'll be okay. Everyone's here. This is Barbara." I kept up some kind of talk, I don't even know what, to connect with him, reassure him.

I looked up to see the rest of my family standing meekly at the foot of the bed, horrified, at what? How bad he looks? My aggressive behavior? I told my mom to get on his other side. I said, "Sing!" And she joined me in "What a fellowship, what a joy divine, leaning on the everlasting arms!" We weren't very good, but his eyes stopped their frantic movement. I got some lotion and massaged his forehead, the only skin exposed. After a while, we moved down and my brothers came up, one on each side. Ken leaned down and said, "Dad, if you don't get better, they're going to sing to you again."

After a while my mother whispered, "There's his doctor!" We cast sidelong glances. He was talking to one of the nurses, looking at a chart. I sensed that none of the others were going to say anything, and I knew that he could leave without talking to us; so I walked toward him, trying to look confident, my underpants in my pocket. My family drew in its collective breath. They wanted so badly to not be any trouble, not get in the way, not confront and risk offending the gods in charge. I could feel them cringing.

I introduced myself and say we'd like a few words when he had a minute. He came right over. They didn't speak to him, but just tried to get out of his way, "Oh, excuse me, pardon me." They smiled weak smiles, heads hanging to the side, and almost curtsied. I asked what Dad's chances were.

"Well, it's hard to say."

I asked if he'd ever seen someone in this shape make it.

"Oh, yes! If his white blood count stays down and no fluid accumulates in his lungs, he stands a pretty good chance."

Whew! "When will we know?"

"The next couple of days will tell."

"Thank you, doctor" (all chimed in on the thanking). We went home with at least some hope.

In the morning his white blood count was up and fluid was accumulating in his lungs, so we knew that hope was gone. The next thing would be funeral plans.

I still puzzle over what took place that day in the I.C.U. Do we really believe that those in power (doctors, teachers, preachers, God) are so capricious and testy that our best chance of survival is to lie low, sit in the last pew, wear beige, stay out of their way and obey all the rules?

And, if so, how is it that Dad died, even though we didn't bring any food into the waiting room? And I wonder. Did those pizza-eaters' dad make it?

. . . . . .

Worthy

> As I believe, I am told and let myself be told that my Creator is gracious, that he is on my side—I do not really know why, but he tells me so and I believe it—and that I am therefore highly pleasing to him just as I am.
>
> —Karl Barth

IT WAS PAST MIDNIGHT, two days before my son's wedding in South Carolina. We had several guests at our house from the United States and overseas, but I was in Florida because my dad was dying. I was in bed and overcome with terror. I couldn't reach my husband by phone because he was staying at a neighbor's house to make room for our guests. So I called my friend, Nancy. She asked what I was afraid of, but I couldn't say. In part, I was afraid my dad would die with no reconciliation between us.

My dad had been chronically depressed and withdrawn from all of us for nearly twenty years. The times he came out of himself were few and far between. I didn't dread losing him as a pillar of strength, a father involved with me or a grandfather to my sons, because he hadn't been those in years, if ever. There would be no "empty chair" at our family gatherings. But I had hoped for some understanding between us and had tried everything I could think of to no avail. Now it was too late. The only thing working was the machines.

Nancy said, "You've been a good daughter." Her assurance and prayers released my fear and put me into such a deep sleep that I couldn't even hang up the phone or turn off the light. I felt someone else do it. I went down, down, floating away from the horror. A gathering of some kind was rocking me and singing to me—high, sweet songs in some strange tongue. If I began to come back up into consciousness, they would rock me down again, singing all the while. Birds? Angels? Judy Collins clones? They were calling me a name, but

. . . . . .

I couldn't make it out. Then I heard it. "Worthy." They were calling me "Worthy." And I let them.

My dad had to have a tube in every orifice before I had the chance to say what I wanted to say. "I love you. I'm proud of you. It's okay." His barrage of complaints, warnings, pessimism were plugged up for good. His motto, "You can't win," was silenced. Had I heard it as a warning or curse? It didn't matter. He was wrong. I was Worthy.

Nancy's words helped me then and help me still. She told me she experiences her dad as a better dad now than when he was alive, because now she knows he sees her through Jesus' eyes. He sees when he hurt her and is sorry, knows he's forgiven. He can look back on the times when she hurt him and forgive her because, like the Lord, he understands.

Once I asked a therapist how I was going to cope with my parents' deaths since the alienation seemed so entrenched and inevitable. She said, "You'll grieve twice, once for the parent you lost and once for the parent you never had." What she didn't tell me was that another way is possible: the grace of having a parent one with the Lord, being, finally, the parent he or she was unable to be in this life. Now I can feel loved, protected and cherished as I never was until my dad and the Father became one. I think of them now as The Ones Who Know the Whole Story.

Dad's Funeral

MOM CALLED ABOUT NOON to say Dad was dying. She also said she wasn't going back over to the hospital. "There isn't anything I can do anyway." She called again later to say he was dead. He'd had a ruptured ulcer with an infection and it had been removed too late. So we made our travel arrangements.

I guess if Dad's life could be summed up in one word, it would be disappointed. His mom died in childbirth when he was ten. He was responsible for the four younger siblings and even for earning grocery money when things were tight for his dad, a carpenter. He began studies for many professions— medicine, law, ministry, but something always defeated him. One day in med school, he was taking an injured man upstairs to surgery. Someone stopped the elevator door and put the man's severed arm on the gurney. Dad fainted, and that was the end of a career in medicine. Then he went to seminary, was ordained and sent to Kentucky as a home missionary to establish rural churches. But when my mom needed several surgeries, they left that work to pay off the bills. He went to work for General Motors "temporarily" in 1947, for thirty years.

There is a special poignancy to having failed at the ministry. You can drop out of law school, and nobody will know; but if you're ordained, it's forever. Once a Reverend, always a Reverend. Did God make a mistake or you? Was the church mistaken to ordain you? Somehow his daily sacrifice of going to the factory job that was so far beneath him meant we were supposed to be unceasingly grateful that he did this to provide for us. And, of course, we weren't. Then, in his late fifties, he retired to Florida where he was happy for about two months. But by then, he was so chronically depressed that nothing could suit him for long.

Gradually, my dad's world had shrunk to his recliner, a state-of-the-art monster with a service contract. The rest of the world had become too dangerous, too painful. Kroger had a slippery floor. The movie seats hurt his hemorrhoids, and restaurants smelled of smoke, even in the no smoking section. Who knew what you could catch these days from bowling shoes? And don't even get him started on church. When I asked his doctor if he'd ever seen anyone in this condition recover, he said, "Oh, yes!" But I don't think Dad put up much of a fight. When I spoke to him to entice him back, I tried to name something he would enjoy if he got better. And drew a complete blank. I couldn't think of a single thing he still enjoyed. So I just made up stuff I would enjoy, if I were he—getting out of the hospital, feeling fresh air on his face, sitting on the porch with a cup of coffee, watching a sitcom on TV. But it was no use.

It was Mom's Baptist minister who came to talk to us, and he'd never even met Dad. What did we want for a funeral? It was to be at a funeral home, not a church. Mom didn't want any part of this discussion, so she left the room. It was all evidently too much for her, so she just left it up to us. Whatever we decided would be it. The minister turned to me and my brothers for suggestions. Nobody said anything. Finally, I said that the Episcopal Church has a liturgy I liked, a prayer for the departed, actively turning the person over to the Lord in love, asking the Lord and the heavenly host to welcome him with joy and thanksgiving. I got out my Book of Common Prayer and found the place. The Celebrant says, "Into your hands, O merciful Savior, we commend your servant (Name).... Acknowledge...a sheep of your own fold, a lamb of your own flock, a sinner of your own redeeming."

It seemed like an act of faith, so we could let go and trust the Lord with this person, transfer him over and, somehow, in the giving up, keep.

My younger brother, Jim, was sitting next to me on the sofa, out of my line of vision, so I jumped when he burst in. "We will have no *literature*!" His face was sweaty and beet red. "My father is in heaven today because he was a born-again Christian. Not because of good works, but because he'd accepted Christ as his personal Savior. And everyone at this funeral will know that and will have the chance to do the same, to come forward and accept Christ as their personal Savior! We'll have no literature!" During the tirade, the minister kept casting nervous glances in my direction, and I nodded assent. That's good; that's fine; yes, that's how it will be. Yes, yes ....

Did my youngest brother, Ken, have any suggestions? Not on your life. (He told me later his actual thoughts at that moment. He was hoping Dad would come back reincarnated as a black lesbian mother on welfare.)

I wondered if it would be possible to have some music. We called the funeral home to find out that there was no organ, keyboard, or piano there, just taped Muzak over the public address system. Couldn't we sing one hymn *a cappella*? The minister said he couldn't do that, couldn't carry a tune. I promised I would copy the words to "Amazing Grace," hand them out and start it at the appropriate time. He looked doubtful. Maybe he thought I would be too upset to do it, but I knew better. There would be music.

When the time came, I started the song, and everyone joined in. A woman behind me had a strong, opera-quality soprano, so that went well.

The minister did a masterful job. He said we know that God had prepared a place just for my father in glory, a mansion for him alone, and that we can trust God with his care. Could we say a-men to that? "A-men!" And he reminded us that my dad was in heaven, not by works of righteousness, but by the grace of God, by being born again and accepting Christ as his personal Savior. And if anyone is here today without Christ, please take this time to accept Christ into your heart. The minister said he'd be available to talk to anyone afterward.

My brother, Jim, thought of the funeral as a chance to spread the Gospel, to tell of my dad's faith and invite others in. I wanted to commend Dad to the Lord's care, to picture him at peace, finally in a happy home. Our two wishes turned out to be compatible after all.

. . . . . .

On Caring

I TOOK A LONG TIME learning to listen to my heart. Well, I usually listened when it said, "Care," but not when it said, "Don't care." Or maybe rather, "step aside from this one for now." It was a new thought to me that in my Christian journey there would be times to take care of myself, protect myself, even from someone else's pain. That you can reach a breaking point by spreading yourself too thin, failing to be tender with yourself.

I remember the first time I heard that warning and consciously obeyed. We returned late at night from a brutal trip to visit my son and daughter-in-law in the Philippines in February of 1995, six months after my three-week-old granddaughter's death in August.

The pain in that house in the Philippines was palpable. It hung in the air with the tropical humidity. Steve told me that he had constant dreams of Sayre. She was about three or four years old and was always walking away from him, so that he never got to see her face, just her back. My recurring dream was that I took in film of her to be developed, but kept getting back just long strings of miniature negatives, which I would hold up to the light and squint at, trying to make out the features of her tiny face. He said the horror would hit him so unexpectedly. One day he was in a supermarket with a cart loaded to overflowing, when he just started sobbing and had to abandon his purchases and run out.

The worst part was that Steve, who had always been so loving to me, was distant and cold and critical. Over Christmas, he second-guessed my every decision and every purchase, so that once, when we were shopping together and I saw a wonderful gift in a junk store, I passed it by and drove back later to buy it, not wanting to hear another put-down.

On this visit, the night before our departure for home, Steve and Amy had a dinner party. One guest was a farmer from upstate New York, very conservative, and we disagreed (amicably, I thought) on New York politics. I was a big fan of Nelson Rockefeller, having received a full merit scholarship in the mid-sixties, to finish college with three kids on my lap, at a time when most grants and scholarships were reserved for teeny-boppers fresh out of high school.

Afterward, when we were the only two still up, Steve took me to task and even made a face to show how I looked when I disagreed with someone. The tirade went on and on, every unbecoming thing about me, searingly accurate. I felt all breath and resilience seep out of me so that I couldn't cry or get up to leave or ask for mercy or even a cup of tea. When he finally went to bed, I was still too stunned to cry or move from my chair. I just sat awake, motionless all night, in misery and cold terror. Was I to lose my first grandchild and my son too? (Afterward my friend, Marigold, assured me that I would not, that it was the grief talking; and I think she was right, because the next morning, Steve was jolly and affectionate, as though nothing untoward had happened).

But I came home low and bruised, barely able to function after this confrontation and a grueling thirty-hour flight. It was the middle of the night, and the red answering machine light was flashing. Something told me not to push that button, but I did anyway to hear Nancy Lauber's voice say: "A child of our parish, Benjamin Hutt, was struck by a car on Monday and died today at Egleston Hospital." Before I could even take it in, something inside said: pretend you didn't push the button. Deal with it in the morning. But when morning came, I knew I was never going to deal with Benjamin's death. I couldn't care. I'd been spared his dying and the funeral and would just step aside from the whole tragedy. Others could care. Others could support his mother, Chris, but I was going to have to pass. The thread was too thin.

. . . . . .

Easter in Portugal

Easter has always been good to me. Christmas is chaos and Thanksgiving iffy, but I truly love Easter, and it rarely goes by without some good surprise, a gift of renewal, forgiveness or grace.

I didn't want to be away from home the Easter of 1998, but Bill had won a trip to Portugal. The dates were set, and it would be his last company-paid trip before retirement. The first ten days in three locations, traveling with a group of 150, felt like an insurance convention, complete with banquets, awards and meetings. The country itself slid by on the other side of the bus window. People said things to each other like, "This bacon is *different!*" Bill and I looked forward to traveling around on our own after the business part of the trip was over.

On Good Friday, we were trundled aboard our three buses to an ancient city high on a steep mountainside. Obidos is walled and compact, laundry flapping on rooftops and geraniums hanging down a couple of stories; nasturtiums grow wild. It was almost noon, and I wanted some time alone for this special day. I couldn't bear to spend the hours Jesus was on the cross at another tourist luncheon in the castle keep.

So I took my leave about eleven-thirty in the morning and arranged to meet Bill and the group around one. I didn't see any evidence of a ceremony, just some religious music wafting out of open windows from various radios all apparently tuned to the same station. I found what looked like the main church. The place was deserted. I went in and knelt on the wooden bench, but there was no prayer book, no rosary to jump-start my devotions.

A gangly teenager came in with an old sheet, followed by a yappy little dog. He noisily dragged a table over the stone floor and stopped in front of the statue of Christ on the cross. He climbed up to cover the statue, but it was too high, half-way up the vaulted ceiling. He got a long pole and tried that, but still fell far short of his goal. He also nearly fell off the table. He saw the dog and yelled at him, sending it scurrying back down the aisle and out of the church. An old priest ambled by to supervise, and soon other old folks drifted in to watch, the dog bouncing in among their ankles, curious too. It looked like a slow day in Obidos. The priest shooed the dog out this time and a chair was added to the top of the tippy table.

I'd read that this church is at least 800 years old. Wouldn't you think they'd have this down by now? Is there no ladder? What should be a solemn rite had become a comedy of errors. There! The head was covered and then one arm; then it all fell down. People shook their heads, pointed and made suggestions. A second chair was added, and this time the dog brought a friend. Both arms got covered, but only half a face. Another swoop and all was finally covered except one pierced, peeking-out hand. Each time he put the sheet over the pole and hurled it upward, the tower of furniture rocked. An old lady with a kerchief on her head whisked her broom at the dogs' retreating bottoms. I looked at my watch. It was twelve-thirty. Jesus is on the cross and I'm watching a three-ring circus. My knees gave out; I sat back and enjoyed the show.

By Easter day we were on our own, and I was very sick with bronchitis. It hurt to breathe. But I doggedly managed find the only church with an English-speaking service. We got lost, and, by the time we arrived, it was just letting out. Sitting on a bench in the lovely park across from the church, I lost it and began to sob. There will be another Mass, but in Portuguese. I thought I'd rather do nothing this sacred morning than go to an impersonal Mass recited by bored clergymen, surrounded by droning strangers getting their weekly tickets stamped. Bill suggested we try it, sit in the back and leave whenever we want. When I found a fresh packet of tissues in my purse, I agreed to give church a try. When we entered, we saw that the only empty seats were half way up, but I knew at once we wouldn't want to leave early.

. . . . . .

The church was aglow. A young people's orchestra played up front, and a white-robed choir stood in the balcony. Small children retrieved, hand over hand, a basket full of Alleluias they'd "buried" for Lent, hung up high, nearly to the ceiling. They gave out butterflies, be-ribboned bits of colored tissue paper from the cocoon of the basket. The congregational singing was heartfelt and full-throated. The peace was passed with eye contact and generous two-handed handshakes.

This time my tears were gentle and cleansing. And my prayers of gratitude included the anxious insurance agent from Kansas examining his first piece of foreign bacon and the motley crew in Obidos doing their best with a pole and a bed sheet. They taught me two things: that you can't schedule a spiritual experience and, when it comes to getting a church ready, dogs are not really all that much help.

A Word for Ron

WE ALL KNEW HE WAS DYING and that this would probably be his last trip to church. He and his wife and toddler always occupied the aisle seats on the second row, left of center. It was typical of Ron to be up front in everything he did, in it with both feet. Bam! "Ron's here!"

The joy of his life, Eric, had been just two when Ron was diagnosed with cancer, and now he was four. He'd never really known his dad not sick. Recently, Debby told me, when his dad fell asleep in the middle of the day, he'd come and ask her, "Is he dead now?"

Somehow Ron got even funnier as he got sicker. His humor took a dark turn but still reflected his childlike view of the world, a skewed take that included an alter ego, Bunky the Clown. Bunky's prized pet was a trained flea, invisible, but a magnificent acrobat for all that.

The last time I visited Ron, he was in a hospital bed in his living room. I'd baked some banana nut bread and brought it warm. At the last minute, while mixing the batter, I threw in a bowlful of leftover blueberries. I held it under his nose, and he said, "Oh, yum! I want some now." Debby was in the shower, so I foraged around in the kitchen for a knife, cut a piece and brought it to him.

"What is it?"

"Banana nut bread."

"But it's blue!" I told him about the last-minute addition.

"Great idea! I mean, what's it going to do—*kill* me?"

Now he'd come to church in his wheelchair, just turned forty and shrunken like an old man. I remember when the test results kept canceling hope on every front, the thing I held on to was Ron's size, not just in spirit, but sheer bulk. He was such a huge guy, filling the doorway. I thought: this'll never get him.

. . . . . .

Ron and I had cancer surgery on the same day. We'd gotten to be good friends putting on a "prom" at church. We visited each other's hospital rooms and joked that cancer must be caused by crepe paper.

Then every test I had came back clear, and everything they tried on Ron failed. His cancer marched through every treatment and never missed a beat. I was home free, but it was hard to celebrate while this much younger man, with a little son to raise, was going under.

At church our Rector, Gray Temple, wanted to anoint Ron with oil and have us all pray for him one last time. He invited Ron's friends to come forward and lay hands on him. By the time I got there, he was surrounded; so I prayed on the periphery, touching the touchers. Afterward, as I walked back to my seat, Gray asked, "Does anyone have a word for Ron?"

Did I hear that right? What a strange request! What can you say to a dying man? Puzzled, I stopped and turned halfway round. My feet still pointed toward the pew, but my top was turned toward the front of the church. I had a distinct impression come up from my twisted middle. It was a picture of Ron as a perfect newborn in the arms of his adoring heavenly father. But courage failed me, and I kept silent. Nobody spoke.

Later I told Ron what I'd seen. But it was too late. The moment had passed. Ron and the congregation had been cheated at a pivotal moment when the divine intersects the human. The overall impression was that the Spirit had nothing to say, had turned her back on Ron. "Cancer? Terminal? Hey, we got nothing!"

If all virtues, raised to their highest purity, become courage, maybe all sins have at their deepest core cowardice. I've known repentance many times in my life but clearly not enough. This time it felt a whole lot like one of those sniveling lepers, newly healed, who went bowling instead of following the Lord with praise and devotion. This one would leave scar tissue.

· · · · · ·

What now? Will I be given another chance at being point guard, the one who will dependably and faithfully hand over the ball? Every Sunday we ask for words of wisdom to encourage people to go for prayer. Some speak out. Others confirm what the last person said. I sit and listen. I'm ready. And I'll do it the next time, obey the nudge, speak out. But will I get the chance? I strained for a while, expectant, head cocked, leaning forward. But God wasn't impressed. So now I just sit and wait. But I'm ready. I'm ready.

. . . . . .

Keys, September 5, 1999

IN THE MIDDLE OF THE SERMON, our priest tells us to take our keys in hand and repeat after him. "In Jesus' name, be released." He asks us to try this in the coming week and gives an example of how it might work.

Recently a woman at a check-out counter, spotting his clerical collar, began explaining why she was a Presbyterian now, not an Episcopalian anymore. She was anxious to tell her story, give her excuses. When it went on a long while, he sensed that she had a burden that went beyond the switching of denominations and said, "In the name of Jesus, be released from being an Episcopalian." Bingo.

Why keys? First of all, keys are ever present and solid, a sort of multi-purpose rosary. They give you a visceral sense of power: unlocking doors, starting cars. And people need the kind of release that Jesus' name can give them. We're usually just reluctant to intercede. So the priest urges us to be ready, to look for the chance to do something similar and, with the keys as a reminder, release someone in Jesus' name.

On Tuesday I have a meltdown. Worn out from months of chronic hip pain, no end in sight, no help from doctors, I panic, decide even the spots on my feet show some massive disease, some sinister, secret deterioration. Maybe the cancer has recurred. As usual, I force myself to keep to routine, swim at the "Y," even though I haven't slept.

But I can't pretend any more. The water is cold, and my body doesn't adjust and I start to shake. No matter how hard I swim, I can't warm up. I pull myself out of the pool, shower and dress. I sit in my car, still shaking and dizzy.

I take my car keys in my hand and repeat aloud a prayer against the rising tide of fear. "In Jesus' name, be released." Nothing. Breathe. Try again. Nada. Maybe this only works on other people.

. . . . . .

Is it even safe to drive? Maybe not; but I can't sit here forever. I start to drive home but go instead to church. It's Tuesday morning; the church office will be packed. Can I get to the right person in time without fainting or breaking down? Donna is in her office, and I plow through and ask if Ceci, our Associate Rector, is there. She is not. I can see by Donna's expression how bad I must look. She draws me into her office and shuts the door. "Wait here. I'll get Kathy."

I don't remember what happened next, just a lot of crying and prayer and grief. Afterward, Kathy says, "Go to bed. You're exhausted."

"But I have a luncheon meeting."

"Set the alarm."

I drive home feeling twenty pounds lighter and sleep from ten-thirty until twelve-thirty, go to my meeting and come home and sleep all afternoon. Where did all that sleep come from? My hip still hurts, but I feel renewed, my feet (without spots), back on the ground.

The key exercise in my car didn't release me from panic or pain. But it did release me from something even bigger: my huge, inbred bug-a-boo, fear of making a scene, interrupting, asking for—no, *demanding*—prayer, putting myself and my needs forward, showing another my utter despair and helplessness.

I recall later Donna running after me as I left the church. Ceci is available now; do I want to see her? No, thanks. If you've seen one Christian, you've seen them all.

. . . . . .

Education for Ministry

I DECIDED TO TAKE THIS COURSE, a four-year study program, because I liked the teacher and the textbook. It was a sort of lay seminary for Episcopalians, a condensed look at theology without Greek and Hebrew. The first year covered the Old Testament, the second the New Testament, the third church history and the last year church doctrine and current issues. My experience of church had been so limited that I wanted an overview of the Bible and church history. What I didn't realize was that this course was primarily, at least under this teacher, an exercise in building Christian community.

The class was a diverse lot, to say the least, from a woman my age who received direct revelation on a regular basis, to a young woman who wasn't even sure she was a Christian, the full range from far-right to left-wing. I took for granted that if the group were a success, over time we would gradually come together, or at least closer, toward some point near the middle, because I thought that Christian community meant consensus. Of course, this turned out not to be the case at all. At the end of our time together, we were no closer about doctrinal issues than we had been at the start. If anything, having taken a fresh look at it all, we were more diverse. But somewhere along the line, we became a community. It was a mystical process and probably better left unexamined, but a few elements were apparent to us all: Bible study, spiritual autobiographies and theological reflections.

The approach to studying the Bible was what I once would have termed liberal. The teacher and text presented various views of, for instance, the first covenant between people and God. It might have been here or there. It might have happened this way or that, to Moses or someone else. It could have been during this time period or another. But, as the teacher said over and over throughout the course, "Something happened!" Something so wild and powerful that it changed the course of human history, reverberating down to this

. . . . . .

112

circle of people sitting around a table in a church library. The touch of God was upon us, a bargain had been struck, a promise made. A spark of a relationship was born. And the liberal view, that we couldn't nail down the covenant, or any of the Bible, to an exact certainty, meant we had to work very hard at staying in the tension, ready to rethink and listen and respect.

Two of us were especially reticent to volunteer our spiritual autobiographies, delaying until we were the only two left. Jim finally allowed that, as uncomfortable as it is to bare your soul, it was getting even more uncomfortable not to do it. "I'm beginning to feel like the only person in the nudist camp wearing clothes." So he volunteered to go next. "But I'm keeping my tie on."

I dreaded my turn even more as I heard the others' stories. They were rich and varied; but most had a fairly clean theme of spiritual redemption, and mine did not. Those who hadn't been born into a Christian home or had only nominal church affiliation, often tied all their troubles to not knowing Christ. Then somewhere he or she became a Christian and looked back with longing. If only they'd been raised in a Christian home, things would have been so much better. Those who had been raised as Christians still had problems, but they were always less traumatic and entrenched. Some lives seemed nearly ideal with both Christian commitment and happy marriages and childhoods. My life didn't fit any of these patterns. When your dad and husband both have "Reverend" in front of their names, even your "down" parts are enmeshed in Christianity. So when I tell the truth, reading from a paper, I look up to see horrified faces.

As the year went on, however, most of the family albums changed shape. One man's father was a clergyman who had such a serious crisis of faith that he put the whole family in harm's way. One woman was an incest victim, and another had a son serving a life sentence. Most of the journey stories were amended and grew in complexity. This brave

· · · · · ·

candor forged a bond of respect and affection, and we got to know the many ways God works to grow and prune—to woo and win.

The last element on the class agenda was a "theological reflection." Someone would tell of an incident from the preceding week: a dream, a snippet overheard, an event that stood out, even though it often seemed insignificant. One was about a man's recent experience bike riding and remembering the bike of his childhood. We all had vivid recollections of favorite bikes, down to the color and brand, the feel of the saddle, the freedom and power a two-wheeler represented. Pedal slowly. Coast along. Full steam ahead, legs pumping and the neighborhood flew past your peripheral vision. Then suddenly and without warning, the chain would slip. Pumping was useless. Soon, as mysteriously as it had disappeared, the chain clicked back into place, and you were on your way.

We each remembered, as children, the times when we pedaled hard to no avail, late to the birthday party, even though we were doing our best. And, as adults, the marriage we worked at with all our might right up to the final court date. Then the work of grace that came out of nowhere when we weren't even trying.

Along with the Bible studies and spiritual autobiographies, these weekly reflections touched on universal themes, leveling the playing field and bringing down what few barriers were left. There would be no consensus, no agreement on doctrine. But, as in the church at large, we would be a community because "something happened."

A Vigil for the Reserved Sacrament
March 2000

IT'S THE MIDDLE OF THE NIGHT, and I awake before the three o'clock alarm. I've laid out jeans, a turtleneck and underwear in the guest room so as not to wake Bill. What do you wear to a vigil? I think of Aunt Bea on *The Andy Griffith Show* wondering what to wear when she was called for jury duty. "Something somber I should think!"

During the Maundy Thursday service extra bread and wine are consecrated for Good Friday and we have each signed up for a spot in an overnight vigil to watch over the reserved sacrament.

Outside, it's calm and dark and mild. I really don't need this jacket, but my snack, gingersnaps, are in the pocket and I've left my purse at home. I drive down deserted roads to the church. I don't think I've ever done anything like this before, kept a vigil, but somehow it feels familiar, seems right to watch over the elements, to watch and pray and not sleep. It feels respectful, acknowledging this night in history, this mystical milestone when the bonds of death will soon be broken. Attention must be paid. We will hand off the hours in an all-night rally—alert, awake Christians, shoulder to shoulder around the globe.

I wonder, as I approach the candle-lit chapel, what the protocol is. It's a silent vigil. Does that mean we don't even greet each other? Just two others are there. A man in a brown jump suit with the company logo on the breast pocket is absorbed in prayer. The woman looks up, and I automatically whisper, "Good morning."

"Good morning," she whispers back.

The atmosphere is so zizzy, so crackly alive compared to the stillness of the night outside. Is it because the candles make the light dance, keep the air in constant motion? Just the three of us, but the chapel feels full.

. . . . . .

I go to an empty section and see we've spaced ourselves apart, like people do in an elevator. What was I thinking bringing gingersnaps wrapped in waxed paper to a silent vigil? Fasting isn't called for, but quiet raisins in a zip-lock would have been a better idea.

The face of Jesus is covered with a black, translucent veil. The look is almost sinister, dark, brooding, withdrawn. And it occurs to me that although I've spent my whole life in relationship with this God/person, praying to, reading of, wondering about this Jesus, he really is still a stranger to me. And I guess it will always be so. I kneel to pray (again, to this familiar and mysterious friend) then settle back into the cool wooden pew. Well, he may be a stranger, but he's my stranger.

What *is* that hum? Is the air conditioning or heat on? No, the candles aren't flickering. And yet this place has a festive air, not noisy, but certainly not silent.

I wonder how it is that I know nothing of the contemplative side of Christianity. Did it seem Roman Catholic and therefore heretical? In any case, I'm ignorant of meditative ways and wonder how to pass the time. We are all three still, but something is moving in here: swirling, rippling color and form. And there's a definite hum.

I become aware of the columbarium, the resting place for urns of the ashes of people who have died. I think about the people I've known these twenty-plus years whose ashes are here. *Are you here? Are you praying for us?* Is that the hum? Then I think of one in particular, the adult son of a friend of mine who took his own life. I've always wanted to tell him how mad I am at him for what he did, for the pain he left behind. *Are you here? Are you praying for us? Well, I'm still mad at you, so you can start with that.*

I start to build up a head of steam. *We're muddling along the best we can, but you left an awful mess down here. Does it weigh out? Is what you needed to get away from bigger than the years of everyday sadness, the hole we have to walk around without you? How do you see it now? If you have pity on yourself, do you have pity on us too? I don't want to add regret to your back; I just need to contradict you, disagree with you, to declare that life is good, is worth it.* But nothing sticks. I'm trying to light a match in a snowstorm. Tiny, invisible flakes spritz out the spark before it has a chance to ignite. Usually I'm really good at anger. I can gather bits and pieces of resentment into a powerful force, dragging carloads of grievances behind. My words can blister paint. But it all keeps slipping away, dissolving in this champagne around me, not a cloud of witnesses, but more a gentle, bubbly tornado.

The swirling merriness seems to mock me, tweak me affectionately. *Can't weigh; lost the scale. Let it go, little sister. It's okay. More than okay. Sit back and let us buoy you up, carry you awhile. Float a minute. Let shame and blame settle to the bottom with your own cowardice and regret. Come play with us. You're it! Leave it all behind. But bring the gingersnaps....*

· · · · · ·

Church, the Rules of the Game

EVERY FRIDAY NIGHT my grandparents came over to play Rook with my parents. On the label pasted underneath the card table was a picture of this very model table supporting five portly bearded men who stood on a board across the top. I would lie under the table and stare at it while the adults played cards.

Who were these men? They're all dressed up in suits and ties. Are they going to a funeral? Prayer meeting? Are they brothers? They look alike. Maybe they're quintuplets, like the Dionnes. Why do they all have long beards? Are they Amish? Jewish Orthodox? The other Smith Brothers who didn't fit on the cough drop box?

And how could such a spindly, collapsible card table made of cardboard (feel it) support all these big men? And how did they get up on that board? First the middle guy, I figured out, then the two immediately in front and back of him. Then the last two, on the ends of the board that hang over the edges. They would have to step on at exactly the same time—one, two, three, go—or the whole thing would come crashing down. Pretty soon I smelled coffee. The game was over.

Rook is a Baptist game—who says Christians can't have fun? We have no truck with traditional playing cards, tools of the devil, with all the overtones of gambling and fortune telling. Rook cards are made for just the one game, the one set of rules, and aren't like regular playing cards. They have four colors instead of four suits, numbered up to fourteen, no face cards, and a Rook, a crow, instead of a Joker. Most non-Baptists have never heard of the game, so it was yet another way in which we were different. "Come out from among them and be ye separate." Being separate—different—was a way, the only way, really, of being holy. And holiness naturally sets you apart from the World even when you're playing cards. Someone would notice—there was just something about you—and that would be a fine chance to witness.

This never actually happened to me, of course, because I was never very good at coming out from among them. In fact, I always liked them. My friends were bright, funny, but not Baptists. Mostly they were Methodists. And there was no evil in them. In their company, I was sometimes ashamed of my Baptistness. Like when I was in the fifth grade, my mom was president of the PTA and organized against square dancing in gym. She prevailed, and we were saved from the evils of do-si-do.

But if the emphasis is on discerning the difference between the true faith (ours) and heresy (often well-intentioned, but fatally flawed nonetheless), the skills you develop in relating to others are divisive, not conducive to finding common ground. As a result, some of my more fervent Christian friends, in their zeal to be pure and untainted, eventually elited themselves right up out of even the most fundamentalist churches. Dropped out completely. Churches were all so corrupt that the truly enlightened ones got to sleep in on Sundays. So Kevin in Norfolk, Virginia, didn't teach Sunday school, even with two degrees in Bible and would only read the Bible in the original languages so he could get it pure, untainted by corruptible translators. Sunday mornings, he studies while his children watch cartoons.

And Betty in Fargo, North Dakota, has two children, seven and nine, who can't read. What with running the yarn shop, she doesn't have time to home school them right now, but there is no way she can let them go to public school and become secular humanists. And the only Christian school in town—to which the children have been offered scholarships— uses a certain curriculum that she has some quibble with. So her kids watch videos in the storeroom. First these devout Christians turned away from the worldliness of poker, narrowed their lives down to Rook. But the narrowing-down momentum carried them so far that they've just turned in their chips, won't even come to the table. Solitaire Christians.

So here's what I think about being holy and separate: I'll pass, thank you. I don't want to be different, discriminating, scrutinizing. I want to be connected, full of mercy as God is full. I don't want to play "Who's Who" every time I meet someone new. I want to take for granted people are good and fine and trustworthy, believers, even, unless they put real effort into proving otherwise. I want to be a part of the church worldwide, one with German Christians who drink beer and Christian Southerners who smoke and Christians— everywhere—who dance. I want to read the same Scripture as many other believers every day and then again on Sunday, some from each section, instead of depending on the whim of a preacher or myself. Not by mood nor by wind shift, but by protocol, saith the church. I want the order of the worship service to be according to the Book of Common Prayer and seasonal emphasis by the liturgical calendar so that we generally cover all the bases most of the time. I want to leave behind the baggage of spiritual discernment and go to an Orthodox cathedral on a Greek Isle, a church in a Welsh fishing village, a chapel in the Black Forest and take my place, be one with whoever else comes to the table. I want to join the parade on any given Sunday toward wherever there's a cross, sit shoulder to shoulder with the devout and the still-undecided, worship together and ask for God's common blessing, be ready for that rare occasion when the divine intersects the temporal. I want the ritual to be familiar even if the language is not.

I guess you could say I want to play the wobbly game of church with traditional playing cards instead of Rook—line up with other Christians like those sweet, trusting brothers on the top of the card table. I want to play with the saints dealt in, giving dead people a vote so we don't have to start each game from scratch.

Are we playing with a full deck here? Are Jokers wild in the deck of this decade? We'll argue over the rules of the game: sexuality, political diversity, authority, the ethics of genetic engineering, whatever those wild ones bring into play. Put all our cards on the table. Shuffle. Cut. Re-deal. But our arguments will end with, "See you in church!"

Who dealt this mess? What's trump? In or out. I'm in. I'm in. Put yer money where your mouth is. Ante up. Keep the faith, but change your mind. Shut up and deal. I'm in. You in? I'm in. I'm in.

. . . . . .